GHOSTS OF SLEEPY HOLLOW

GHOSTS OF SLEEPY HOLLOW

HAUNTS OF THE HEADLESS HORSEMAN

SAM BALTRUSIS

Haunted America

Published by Haunted America
A Division of The History Press
Charleston, SC
www.historypress.com

Copyright © 2024 by Sam Baltrusis
All rights reserved

First published 2024

Manufactured in the United States

ISBN 9781467158022

Library of Congress Control Number: 2024937580

Notice: The information in this book is true and complete to the best of our knowledge. It is offered without guarantee on the part of the author or The History Press. The author and The History Press disclaim all liability in connection with the use of this book.

Woodcut illustration of the Headless Horseman from Washington Irving's "The Legend of Sleepy Hollow." *Illustration courtesy of xochicalco from Depositphotos.*

CONTENTS

CONTENTS

FOREWORD

Despite its quiescent name, the village of Sleepy Hollow, New York, is a crowded warren of bustling buildings, packed with people and clogged with cars. That's because it's a short drive from Manhattan, strung along Route 9 (aka Broadway), a sluggish road that eventually heads to the city to hit it big in the theater.

However, if you look closer at this suburb of New York City near the southern tip of the Hudson Valley—and you don't even have to look that close, honestly—you'll discover something strange. A single image is repeated everywhere—on the shields of its first responders, on the sides of its recycling bins, on the T-shirts and mugs and magnets of its gift shops, on the murals of its main strip, on its street signs.

Sleepy Hollow is covered in monsters—well, one monster: the Headless Horseman.

The village is where Washington Irving set his 1820 story "The Legend of Sleepy Hollow." Today, you can still trace the route where the headless Hessian chased Ichabod Crane, starting at the site where British spy John André was captured during the Revolutionary War (today a memorial) all the way over the famous bridge (today a short stretch of multi-laned asphalt) and finally to the Old Dutch Church that still stands today, presiding over the graveyard where the headless specter "tethered his horse nightly."

Nearby, in the adjoining Sleepy Hollow Cemetery, is the grave of Irving himself, who moved to the area toward the end of his life, triply consecrating it with his story, his presence and his bones.

Sleepy Hollow has embraced its spooky literary heritage. A herd of Headless Horsemen runs through the village daily across signs and surfaces. The local high school mascot is the Headless Horseman. Businesses are themed according to the cabeza-less canterer. An eighteen-foot-tall sculpture of the Horseman chases Ichabod down Broadway. And the village throws a mean Halloween, always themed with its favorite galloping ghoul.

They love their Headless Horseman in Sleepy Hollow.

I get it. This fiend without a face is my favorite monster of all the monsters that I have loved in my life. I think it's because of his inextricable connection to my favorite season, autumn, and my favorite holiday, Halloween.

The "Welcome to Historic Sleepy Hollow" sign greets passersby heading down Broadway. *Photo by Sam Baltrusis.*

And sure, that swatch of calendar is completely monster-mashed. However, you can have witches any month of the year. (They have their own calendar, after all.) Dr. Frankenstein can raise a creature from the dead anytime. (Body parts are always in season if you know where to dig.) Vampires need blood year-round.

The Headless Horseman of Sleepy Hollow only works against a backdrop of fire-colored leaves in October. Only works propelled by chill winds after the fireplace warmth of harvest parties. Only works with a pumpkin tucked under his arm. After all, who wants a Headless Horseman holding a grinning watermelon? Or a carrot-pierced snowball?

But there is another level to Sleepy Hollow. And for this one, you do have to look a lot more closely. You must look below the expensive condos of this commuter town. You must look beneath the cape and saddle of the Horseman himself.

There you'll find a Sleepy Hollow populated by all kinds of lore, all the creepies that haunt its history and would rule the nights and Halloweens in any other village, a stratum of ghosts and witches and devils that was a big reason Irving set his tale in this hollow in the first place. It just so happens that all the ghosts and banshees and things with horns and saucer eyes in Sleepy Hollow are subjugated by the singular specter of the Headless Horseman, who reigns them all as the supreme spook.

The Old Dutch Church of Sleepy Hollow is listed on the National Register of Historic Places. *Photo courtesy of Lee Snider from Depositphotos.*

Sleepy Hollow has more legends than the "Legend." And Sam Baltrusis is here with this book to unearth them from the byways so well-trampled by the Horseman's hooves—with the appropriate obeisance made to the phantom rider, of course. Because even though a single scary tale made Sleepy Hollow the place it is today, it is a place of many scary stories.

J.W. Ocker is the author of macabre travelogs, horror novels and spooky children's lit, as well as creator of the website OTIS: Odd Things I've Seen.

Visit JWOcker.com for more information.

ACKNOWLEDGEMENTS

While I was writing *Ghosts of Sleepy Hollow*, the unthinkable happened. The apartment above mine mysteriously caught on fire one morning and set off the alarms and sprinklers in my home.

Almost everything I owned was destroyed—including most of the handwritten notes and original research that I had printed out for this book—by the intense water damage unleashed from above. Oddly, I was writing the section about the Bronze Lady of Sleepy Hollow Cemetery and the alleged curse she inflicts on visitors who disrespect her when my life quickly turned upside down.

I had visited the statue a few weeks before the fire with my psychic-medium friend April Busset. Soon after my extreme bad luck, she also had a freak accident happen at her home in New Jersey, with a tree falling during a thunderstorm and piercing a hole in her roof.

Did we somehow upset the Bronze Lady?

Convinced that we were cursed, April and I met up for one last time to hopefully make amends with the hex-inducing statue. During our first visit to Sleepy Hollow Cemetery, we found her by haphazardly driving up a hill and looking out of the car window. It was like she was waiting for us.

The second time around, however, we were lost. We couldn't find the Bronze Lady. It was only a few weeks after our first visit, and we kept whizzing by the Sleepy Hollow Cemetery Bridge hoping we could retrace our previous path. No luck.

After some online sleuthing, we were able to pinpoint her location. As we walked up the hill to give the Bronze Lady a peace offering—a beautiful

The Bronze Lady guards a mausoleum in Sleepy Hollow Cemetery and is considered to be the spellbound region's "other legend." *Photo by Sam Baltrusis.*

crystal stone gifted to me by my dear friend Meg Mahoney, who passed away on May 6, 2023—the energy outside of the mausoleum shifted. It was as if her frown turned into a Mona Lisa smile. Apology accepted?

My medium friend, who is also the founder of *Ghosted* magazine, started to pick up a disembodied presence that emerged from the portal between two trees next to the sculpture commissioned by Samuel Thomas's wife, Ann.

According to Busset, it was the mysterious woman's energy that entered the outdoor space.

"I'm getting that she likes us," she told me. "I'm hearing that what happened to us was a blessing in disguise."

As we closed our impromptu ceremony outside of the Civil War general's crypt, we both felt an overwhelming feeling of peace. Mission accomplished.

I was taken aback by a wave of gratitude not only for all of the fun-filled adventures I had with April but also for many of my peers and friends in the paranormal community who helped make *Ghosts of Sleepy Hollow* a reality, including Alex Matsuo, Andrew Warburton, Brian J. Cano, Christopher Rondina, Leanna Renee Hieber, Joni Mayhan, Richard Estep, Ron Yacovetti and master storyteller Jonathan Kruk. His research inspired the spooktacular "Ichabod Crane's Race" map illustrated by Joe Diebboll from The Highland Studio.

For the record, watching Kruk's performance of "The Legend of Sleepy Hollow" at Washington Irving's Sunnyside on Halloween night was a dream come true for me. The experience was pure magic.

Special thanks to J.W. Ocker, author of *The New York Grimpendium*, for writing the book's foreword and agreeing to do a last-minute interview at the Sleepy Hollow Hotel. It felt like the spirits of the Hudson Valley kept putting him in my path—even though we're both based in New England—while writing this book. I loved every odd minute of it.

Angela Artuso from Gotham Paranormal deserves major props for taking many of the photos and exploring several of the haunts with me featured in *Ghosts of Sleepy Hollow*.

I would also like to thank Banks Smither, who initially commissioned this project and helped map out the book's structure, and Mike Kinsella from The History Press/Arcadia for their support during the process of putting *Ghosts of Sleepy Hollow* together.

And if I don't give a supernatural shoutout to the Bronze Lady, heads are gonna roll.

For those who love Irving and his Headless Horseman as much as I do, this book is for you. Happy hauntings!

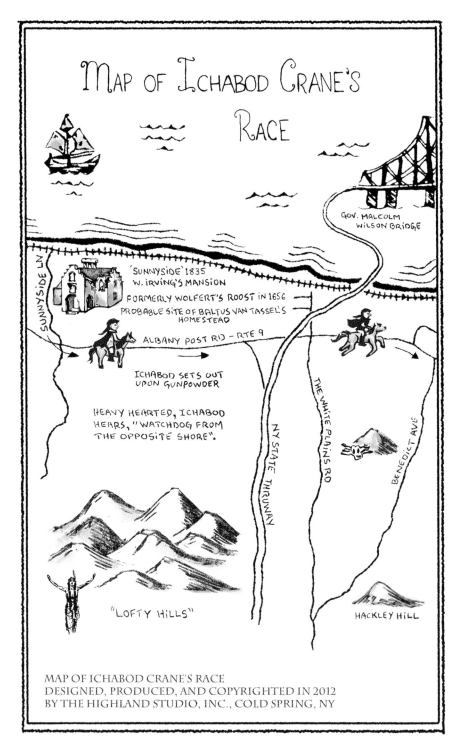

"Ichabod Crane's Race" map inspired by Jonathan Kruk's research in *Legend and Lore of Sleepy Hollow and the Hudson Valley. Illustration by Joe Diebboll from The Highland Studio.*

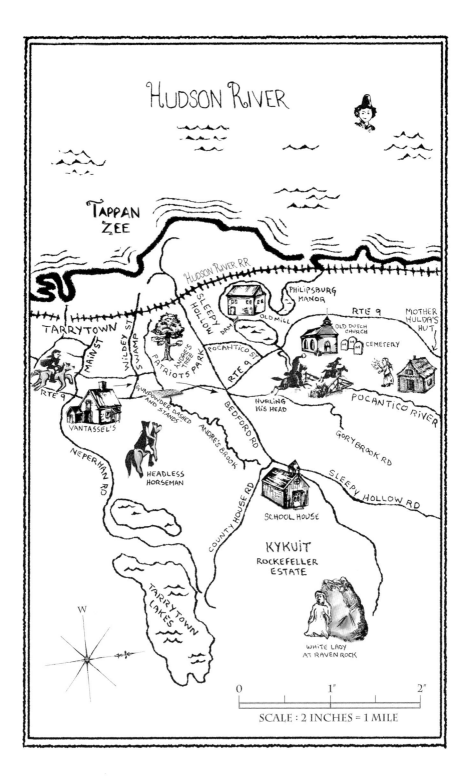

INTRODUCTION

A drowsy, dreamy influence seems to hang over the land, and to pervade the very atmosphere.

—Washington Irving, "The Legend of Sleepy Hollow"

Sleepy Hollow, New York, is brimming with ghostly legends that have somehow taken on a life of their own.

Nestled on the banks of the Hudson River, the fabled region—which includes the adjoining Tarrytown—has become the go-to place during spooky season thanks to the popularity of Washington Irving's "The Legend of Sleepy Hollow."

Late-night lantern tours in search of a decapitated soldier's galloping ghost? Yes, please.

If one spends enough time walking through the labyrinthine paths of the village's historic cemeteries, however, there's something sinister oozing beneath Sleepy Hollow's rustic storybook façade.

It's as if the entire hamlet is under some sort of enchantment. Or, as Irving penned in 1820, it oddly feels like the locals are somehow bewitched and "are subject to trances and visions."

The revered writer referred to the area as the "spell-bound region," and rightfully so. According to several firsthand accounts, creepy music and disembodied voices emerge out of thin air.

Based on Irving's mythical take on his later-in-life hometown, it should be no surprise that the Headless Horseman isn't the Valley's only fearsome phantom seeking postmortem revenge.

Heads roll when the Headless Horseman emerges from the darkness during Sleepy Hollow's annual Halloween celebration. *Photo courtesy of James Kirkikis from Shutterstock.*

The entire region seems to be teeming with paranormal activity. Several publications sensationally claim that both Sleepy Hollow and Tarrytown together make the "most haunted places in the world."

But are they?

After digging beneath the surface, it's difficult to pinpoint what's actually paranormal activity versus a made-up ghost story that has been collectively conjured over a two-hundred-year period.

Alex Matsuo, a Maryland-based author and paranormal investigator who has written about the area's alleged paranormal activity in her *Spooky Stuff* blog, believes that the line between fact and fiction is somehow blurred in Sleepy Hollow.

"After Washington Irving's infamous tale plunged the area into fame, I would hypothesize that perhaps some of the paranormal activity could be attributed to thought-forms," Matsuo told me. "There's also the case of self-fulfilling prophecies that people can accomplish without realizing it."

Matsuo cited the replica of the bridge in Sleepy Hollow Cemetery as a potential hot spot for ghostly encounters that are freakishly fueled by the expectations of thrill-seeking visitors.

"Just by knowing the tale and the true story behind it, they would already get a case of the creeps," she explained. "Then, with tensions rising, they hear a branch break or footsteps, and they get really spooked. They go home and tell their friends and family about the creepy experience, unknowing that there was an animal nearby causing the ruckus."

Also, there are what paranormal researchers call thought-forms or an outward manifestation of the heightened emotions of those who visit Sleepy Hollow during spooky season. Matsuo believes that based on this concept, extreme fear can somehow take a physical form within the spirit world.

"When you have a massive amount of people invested in a story, even a fictional story based on real people, that energy has to go somewhere," she said. "In the case of Sleepy Hollow, it may have manifested into paranormal occurrences. I would guess that most of that energy is more organized, but I wouldn't be surprised if some of that energy was displaced, which could explain some of the random paranormal events that have happened over the years."

Inspired by Matsuo's thought-form theory, I decided to visit the village on All Hallows' Eve in hopes of having an encounter with the hell-raising Hessian. I flew into LaGuardia Airport and then took the commuter rail from New York City. After my train ride, I checked into one of the Valley's notoriously haunted hotels, the Tarrytown House Estate on the Hudson.

Sleepy Hollow Cemetery Bridge during the autumn. *Photo courtesy of BackTrack540 from Shutterstock.*

I wanted to see for myself if the ghosts of Sleepy Hollow came out to play when the veil between the living and dead became thinner. Unbeknownst to me, the most terrifying experience I had that chilly Halloween night was making a trek from one of the fabled region's most haunted locations to another.

Based on the online map, it looked like Washington Irving's Sunnyside was only a stone's throw from my hotel, so I decided to walk to the theatrical reenactment of "The Legend of Sleepy Hollow" led by master storyteller Jonathan Kruk.

In hindsight, the early evening stroll was a bad idea. I should have taken a cab.

As I was heading down the street on foot toward the winding Sunnyside Lane, the Halloween sky turned pitch black. There were no sidewalks leading from Broadway to Irving's home by the Hudson River. I panicked as cars started to pull into the long road and I tried to balance on a jagged stone path to keep out of harm's way. I was wearing all black, and, well, it was difficult to see even when I held up my trusty flashlight that I often use on paranormal investigations.

I hid in the bushes and dodged cars as they passed. I felt like I was living a modern-day version of the classic American tale but instead of a horse, the Headless Horseman was in a Range Rover and he kept chasing me deeper into the darkness.

As each car skimmed by me on the desolate stretch of road, I sheepishly held up my flashlight so passersby could see that I was a pedestrian and not some phantom menace lurking in the shadows.

After I made the trek that night and came to the end of the winding path, I noticed an open gate that seemed to lead to Sunnyside. I gasped for air.

It was the employee entrance, and I quickly scurried up the hill and down the path so I could see Kruk's performance from beginning to end.

The path was muddy and a bit slippery as I maneuvered through the tree-lined thicket. In the distance, I heard what sounded like the "clip-clop" of horse hooves hitting the ground followed by a loud neigh.

Was it Ichabod Crane's horse? I chuckled a bit thinking about the nerdy schoolmaster's four-legged companion named Gunpowder.

As I looked around the property, I started to notice what looked like a shadow figure wearing a hooded cloak. I was in shock, hoping it was merely pareidolia, or the tendency to perceive an image in randomly ambiguous patterns.

I then closed my eyes, praying that the druid-like figure would disappear. When I opened them again, it was still there.

As I scanned the clearing covered in leaves, I noticed that there was more than one fearsome phantom walking around.

I was surrounded.

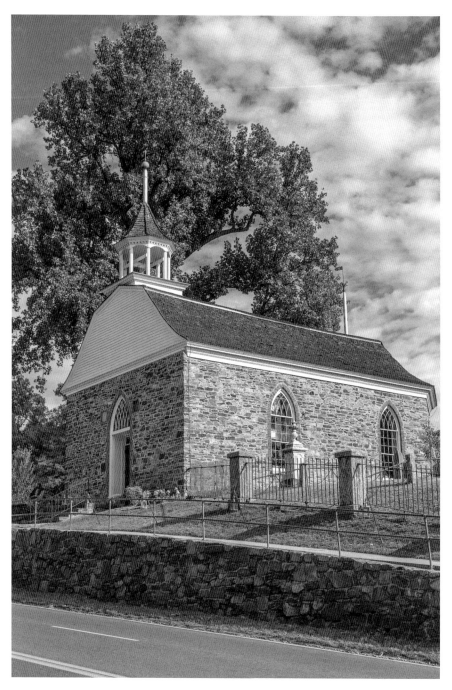

The Old Dutch Church was featured in Washington Irving's "The Legend of Sleepy Hollow." *Photo courtesy of OlegAlbinsky from iStock.*

The modern version of the Headless Horseman holds a jack-o'-lantern. *Illustration courtesy of Daniel Eskridge from Shutterstock.*

My heart started to beat through my chest as I frantically looked around the wooded area to find a way to get inside. I noticed what looked like an outdoor tent with a dim light. I quickly walked through the thicket and jumped up on a stone-lined pathway leading to Washington Irving's former home.

"Excuse me, sir," said what sounded like a female voice. "Can I help you?"

I was breathing heavily at this point as I lifted my head, fully expecting to come face-to-face with one of the wicked wraiths.

"I'm here for the Halloween performance," I said, praying that I was in the right place. I looked over and saw a woman checking for tickets.

"You better hurry," she said as she found my reservation on her computer screen. "They're about to start."

The employee pointed to a dimly lit path that led to a small theater set up outside of Sunnyside. As I crossed a wooden bridge, I saw two of the hooded figures stationed on the hill.

No looking back. I pushed forward hoping they would just go away. I gasped for air.

I could clearly see one of the cloaked men had what looked like a torch-like flashlight.

The village clock is adorned with Halloween decorations welcoming tourists to Sleepy Hollow, New York. *Photo courtesy of demerzel21 from Depositphotos.*

"Watch your step, " he said, pointing to what looked like several rows of chairs.

"Well, at least the Grim Reaper has manners," I thought to myself. I slowly inched past him only to notice that there was an entire clan of them at the end of the path.

It was a motley crew of hooded hellraisers. Help me.

I had a look of terror on my face. As I was about to make a run for it, one of the cloaked men dropped his hood to assist me in finding a seat.

The shadow men weren't sinister spirits. They were in costume and serving as ushers for the evening. I nervously laughed out loud as I quickly made my way to the back row of the outdoor seating.

I survived my All Hallows' Eve adventure at Washington Irving's Sunnyside. Remember the mysterious horse galloping in the darkness on my terrifying trip to the theater? It was an actor on horseback, and he trotted his way to greet attendees after the performance.

On Halloween night, I came face-to-face with the Headless Horseman. And thankfully, I didn't lose my head.

CHAPTER 1
THE LEGEND

More than two centuries after Washington Irving unleashed "The Legend of Sleepy Hollow," the Headless Horseman is still very much alive in pop culture.

Elizabeth Bradley, a historian and author of *Knickerbocker: The Myth Behind New York*, rattled off a few of the various adaptations of the great American ghost story on the October 26, 2022 edition of WNYC News.

"It has such legs and you can see that in all of the different interpretations," Bradley said during the radio interview. "There truly is a version of 'Sleepy Hollow' for every generation." It's an impressive list that includes Disney's animated classic from 1949 and Tim Burton's supernatural horror flick starring Johnny Depp and Christina Ricci.

Of course, no one can eclipse the original, which was initially published with a collection of essays and stories for *The Sketch Book of Geoffrey Crayon, Gent.* in 1820.

"Irving's version of the Headless Horseman is set in the Hudson Valley region, and it pits an outsider, a Yankee, named Ichabod Crane against a very insular Dutch community," Bradley said. "Throughout the course of the story, Ichabod pursues a local Dutch heiress in an effort to integrate himself into this community and is ultimately run out of town by the apparition of the Headless Horseman."

Bradley told WNYC that she believes the famed short-story writer created the headless Hessian in an attempt to populate a young nation with its own ghosts and mythologies. "You have to remember that Irving was born the

The headless Hessian didn't have Halloween-themed props when he pursued Ichabod Crane in the original short story, "The Legend of Sleepy Hollow." *Photo courtesy of Morphart from Depositphotos.*

year after the American Revolution ended," she said. "The war was in the rear-view mirror of the people of Sleepy Hollow and a very new United States. It was an opportunity to create a whole regional culture. He really seized the moment and had a lot of fun with it."

How did "The Legend of Sleepy Hollow" become associated with All Hallows' Eve? Bradley explained that the holiday wasn't even on Irving's radar when he fleshed out America's first monster. "He doesn't mention Halloween once in the story," she said. "[The Headless Horseman] is often associated with having a pumpkin for a head," she added, noting that the character's jack-o'-lantern prop was added in Disney's *The Adventures of Ichabod and Mr. Toad*, and over the years, the haunting imagery then seared itself into pop culture. "Most people only knew the Disney version and that's where the Halloween association really started to come into play," Bradley added.

J.W. Ocker, author of *The New York Grimpendium* and creator of the *OTIS: Odd Things I've Seen* blog, is on board with the idea that the Headless Horseman has somehow become the unofficial ambassador of spooky season. "The Headless Horseman is the spirit of fall," Ocker told me during a sit-down interview at the Sleepy Hollow Hotel. "Every monster wants to be

The title text for a print edition of "The Legend of Sleepy Hollow" found among the papers of the late Diedrich Knickerbocker. *Photo courtesy of Canopic from iStock.*

associated with autumn, but there's something about him running through a forest with the leaves changing colors that makes him the patron monster of Halloween. The bigger Halloween gets, the bigger he gets. Every time you feed Halloween, you feed him."

Ocker agreed with Bradley that the animated version from the Disney movie has become ingrained in the American psyche. "Our generation grew up with the Disney cartoon," he said. "You can't think of the Headless Horseman without thinking of the purple-cloaked, cackling creature from the animated version. The imagery has almost become a part of the monster's brand."

The *United States of Cryptids* author said he always thought the Headless Horseman had a jack-o'-lantern in one hand and a battle sword in another, but he was shocked to learn that Irving didn't include the macabre accessories in the short story. He was also convinced that the Headless Horseman eventually caught up with Ichabod Crane on a covered bridge. Not true.

"People who visit Sleepy Hollow always want to see the covered bridge, but it doesn't exist," Ocker said. "If I could change one thing to the original story, I would make it a covered bridge. It just seems fitting."

Despite being tweaked a bit in the modern adaptations of Irving's story, Ocker said the Headless Horseman is still his all-time favorite galloping ghoul. "Irving gave us the first real American monster," he told me. "I'm not a very patriotic guy, but as an American there's something that speaks to me about the horseman. It's our monster. Frankenstein is from Germany and Dracula is from Transylvania. Thanks to Irving, we have our own."

The secret to the short story's success? Ocker believes the ambiguity of Irving's fearless phantom somehow amplifies its mystique. "All we know is he was a Hessian soldier who lost his head during the American Revolution," he told me. "There's not much of a backstory to him. He's this vague creature that pops up in the graveyard and runs around on his horse. He's not jumping out of your closet. He has no face. He's in essence an invisible man and there's something unnerving about him as a monster."

In *Lore of the Ghost*, Brian Haughton mentioned that Irving was living in Birmingham, England, when he wrote "The Legend of Sleepy Hollow" and surmised that the celebrated American author "probably picked up on some of the elements he used in the story" overseas. "The headless ghost motif was known in German folklore at least as early as 1505 when it was recorded in a sermon written by Geiler von Kaysersberg, who mentions headless spirits being part of the Wild Hunt," he noted.

While Haughton wrote that Irving was strongly influenced by the stories told by Dutch immigrants during his childhood in New York, he suggested that it's also likely that the writer was inspired by the recurring headless ghost motifs from northern European folklore. "The tradition of the headless ghost is found worldwide in many diverse cultures, and exhibits broadly the same characteristics connected with death and death warnings," Haughton reported. "Popular tradition attributes such hauntings to the wandering spirits of those who died by beheading, either by execution or accident."

Haughton is in agreement that Irving's story continues to leave a profound mark on popular culture. "Irving's dark story of the headless Hessian soldier who rides forth every night through the dark lanes of Sleepy Hollow, and the dénouement of the tale involving a supernatural wild chase through the woods, has had a significant effect on the nature of American hauntings," Haughton wrote in *Lore of the Ghost*. "The influence of Irving's tale on popular culture is evident."

Alex Matsuo, author of *Women of the Paranormal*, told me that there may be an underlying reason why "The Legend of Sleepy Hollow"

The Headless Horseman has appeared in several movie adaptations and TV programs, including the series *Sleepy Hollow*. *Photo courtesy of s_bukley from Depositphotos.*

continues to strike a chord with American readers. "We don't think about it often, but there are countless legends that were created to dehumanize a group," Matsuo explained. "Instead of perceiving the Hessian as a real person, granted a terrifying figure during the time of the Revolutionary War, he turned it into this story that is meant to remind people that the Hessians were not meant to be trusted, even after the war was over."

Even though Matsuo sees a deeper meaning to what could be viewed as a cautionary tale, she said the Headless Horseman keeps luring her back to the Hudson Valley area. "Between the story of the Hessian soldier who lost his head around Halloween in 1776, and Ichabod Crane encountering him

Fall foliage on display from the steps of the Sleepy Hollow Cemetery in October. *Photo courtesy of spork_spelunking from Depositphotos.*

while trying to avoid him at all cost, there is a lesson to be learned there," Matsuo said. "But I think the way that Disney commercialized 'The Legend of Sleepy Hollow,' plus the Tim Burton film, there is a romanticization of the spellbound region that has cemented it into Halloween traditions."

CHAPTER 2

THE AUTHOR

There's no denying that Washington Irving was an important American writer, but was his work historically accurate? According to a New York–based author and tour guide, not exactly.

Born on April 3, 1783, to a merchant family, Irving was raised in New York and sent to the Hudson Valley region at fourteen to avoid a deadly yellow fever epidemic that gripped Manhattan. In 1802, he penned a series of observational-style letters published in the *Morning Chronicle* under a nom de plume.

Leanna Renee Hieber, coauthor of *A Haunted History of Invisible Women* and tour guide with NYC's acclaimed Boroughs of the Dead, insisted that she respects Irving's work immensely but pointed out his tendency toward "fancifying New York history."

Hieber said that Irving deserves props for nicknaming the city that never sleeps "Gotham," but he was known to "blur fact and fiction early in his career."

For example, Hieber told me about a hoax Irving orchestrated by placing missing-person ads for his literary alter ego Diedrich Knickerbocker. The made-up character supposedly disappeared after refusing to pay his hotel bill. "People believed Knickerbocker was a real person, going so far as issuing a reward to find him," she explained.

Hieber insisted that "Irving loved his hometown and revered the stunning beauty of the entire Hudson Valley region." She continued, "But Irving's New York was built on legends, folklore and some good-natured skewering, which became wrapped up with the city's real history."

As a child, Hieber said, Irving grew up on William Street near Manhattan's former theater district. "He'd often ditch studies to attend performances, and his early love of plays would inform a great deal of his writing," she said. "During the yellow fever outbreak of 1798, his family sent him upriver to Tarrytown, where local folklore and old Dutch customs amused and intrigued him."

A few years after his literary debut in the *Morning Chronicle*, Irving moved to England to tend to the family business, where he crafted his beloved *The Sketch Book of Geoffrey Crayon, Gent.* during the winter of 1819 and 1820. The collection of short stories catapulted the accidental author to fame thanks to his folktales "Rip Van Winkle" and "The Legend of Sleepy Hollow," which left an indelible mark on the American literary landscape.

Washington Irving was an American short story writer, essayist, biographer, historian and diplomat during the early 1800s. *Photo courtesy of georgios from Depositphotos.*

"He didn't invent the legend of the Headless Horseman," Hieber explained. "He heard the ghost story from the locals. Irving just managed to be the first to craft it artfully for publication, and in his own style. He's a true storyteller of the city and surrounding environs as a whole."

In 1832, he returned to the Hudson Valley and acquired a "neglected cottage" that would become his later-in-life home, Sunnyside.

Hieber said Irving commuted back and forth from NYC to the Hudson Valley and had a flat in the historic Colonnade Row. "The building's marble was mined by convicts at Sing Sing penitentiary north of the city," she explained.

Across the street from Colonnade Row is a "palatial red-brick Romanesque icon that is now The Public Theatre, originally the Astor Library," Hieber said. "It was built as the first major public library in the city, thanks to the Astor family fortune."

She said Irving was hired as one of the executors of the Astors' estate and served as the library's first chairman. The Public Theatre building, Hieber explained, is home to one of her favorite Irving ghost stories in its circulation of tales.

Postcard of Washington Irving's Sunnyside printed in 1909 by Russell & Lawrie. *Courtesy of Card Cow.*

"The first librarian, Joseph Cogswell, friend of the Astors and a man never prone to flights of fancy, was granted an apartment in the library he oversaw," Hieber told me. "Beginning late one night in 1860, Cogswell was shocked to see his deceased friend Austin L. Sands appear among the stacks of books. Sands appeared three nights in a row in the same place. George Templeton Strong, famed city diarist, got hold of the account and soon newspapers were running with stories of the haunted library."

Hieber said Cogswell was "a no-nonsense man undeterred by specters"— and then he spotted another recently departed friend, Washington Irving, who had died in his Hudson Valley home on November 28, 1859.

"Cogswell asked Irving's ghost his business and Irving replied that he was just there to do some research on a project and he wouldn't trouble him anymore once it was complete," Hieber explained. "Good on his word, after a few weeks, his apparition wasn't seen again by Cogswell, though his presence would be noted by other library patrons."

It's important to point out that eight months before he passed away at seventy-six years old, Irving penned a five-volume biography of George Washington. Was he finishing his massive project about the country's first president in the afterlife?

As a fellow author and historian, Hieber joked that she can certainly relate to the feeling of never-ending research, even if it's from beyond the veil.

Washington Irving's family plot in the Sleepy Hollow Cemetery. *Photo by Angela Artuso.*

HEADLESS HORSEMAN

While historians agree that Irving was inspired by the spellbound region's eerie aesthetic and ghostly legends, the true origin of his headless Hessian is still open for debate.

Cristina Lombardi, a tour guide with the Sleepy Hollow Cemetery, told me a story that has been passed down from generation to generation. It involves the real Van Tassels, who were well-known Patriots during the American Revolution. Because of the family's affiliation with the colonists, the redcoats targeted their farmhouse.

"During the middle of the night, the Redcoats forced the Van Tassels out of their home and torched their farmhouse," Lombardi told me while leading a tour through the cemetery. "They burned it to the ground."

A woman—who would have been Katrina Van Tassel's grandmother— was frantically looking for her youngest child while the other family members were all safely gathered on the lawn.

"She believed her baby was in the house and she tried to charge in and save her youngest. But she was physically restrained by a Hessian soldier who would not let her back into the house," Lombardi told me. "He dragged

Mrs. Van Tassel into the woods, which alarmed the family, but she was relieved to find that her baby was unharmed by the fire."

According to Lombardi, the redcoats were furious that the rogue Hessian defied orders. When the Van Tassels went back to what remained of their home, she told me, "they found the decapitated corpse of that Hessian soldier with his head placed on the steps of their torched farmhouse."

Lombardi said the gruesome word-of-mouth tale has been passed down by locals over the years. "It's very probable that Irving would have heard the story during his childhood," she said, adding that "it's also very likely that the story of the headless Hessian informed his famous tale."

Did the Van Tassel family secret inspire Irving? And more importantly, what is a Hessian?

The German mercenaries served among the English forces during the American Revolution, and in several cases, their spirits continue to linger in the afterlife.

The soldiers for hire were strangers in a foreign land. Many of them died tragic deaths, fighting in bloody battles with minimal pay or motivation. Because of their lack of passion for the war they were fighting, would this result in a potential haunting?

Christopher Rondina, a New England–based author and tour guide, thinks it's a viable possibility. He strongly believes they were victims of false promises and suggested that a few of the Hessians are sticking around in search of postmortem justice.

"Many of the Hessian soldiers came here having been promised land in this new, wide-open nation," Rondina told me. "Since so many Hessians had

This marker in Sleepy Hollow Cemetery indicates that the Headless Horseman tethered his horse at night in the churchyard. *Photo by Angela Artuso.*

little chance of bettering their situation in the princedoms of feudal Germany, they pinned their dreams here in the New World. They essentially bet everything on a hollow promise that would never be fulfilled. Many of them died knowing they traveled halfway across the world for nothing."

Rondina noted that the Hessians saw little-to-no money for their services because the British made a deal with the princes who ruled their homeland. "The soldiers received their standard pay, if any, plus food, gear and little else," he said.

It's also important to point out that those who survived the Revolutionary War did end up staying in America. Many of the Hessians were able to assimilate into the German communities that were already settled in Pennsylvania, New York and New Jersey.

The casualties, however, weren't so lucky.

In *Legends of Sleepy Hollow: The Lost History of the Headless Horseman*, Rondina explored the real-life inspirations behind many of the characters featured in Irving's classic, including the ghostly antagonist believed to be a Revolutionary War–era Hessian soldier.

"I learned some fascinating and unexpected facts while researching the story, including a real Ichabod Crane who had served in the military with Washington Irving," he told me. "He wasn't pleased at all with his inclusion in the story."

Rondina's most extraordinary discovery was that a genuine Revolutionary War soldier had been the inspiration for the Headless Horseman legend.

"He was alleged to be a German mercenary working for the British army, but his identity was unknown, even two hundred years later," he said. "I believed the answer to his mystery had to be out there somewhere, so I began digging, looking for any clues to the ghost's mortal existence. The answer was out there, but I had to go to Germany to find it, hidden among centuries-old military records."

Based on his research, Rondina said a real-life tragedy that happened on the battlefield at Merritt Hill in White Plains is what actually inspired Irving. "On a cold November morning in 1776, a mounted Hessian soldier was decapitated by a cannonball at that spot, just as Washington Irving's story says," Rondina confirmed. "The site today is rural and quiet, but the wooded hillside gives off an eerie energy that can't be denied. It's the very site where the Hessian restlessly searches each night for his long-lost head."

The man's name? Heinrich Range.

According to Rondina, he wouldn't be surprised if the soldier's headless specter has haunted the Hudson Valley region for years. "Is it possible that the ghost of Heinrich Range truly does ride out in search of his head along the dark, wooded roads between White Plains and Sleepy Hollow? Perhaps so, if one is inclined to believe in such things," he wrote.

As the author pointed out in his *Legends of Sleepy Hollow* book, the decapitated soldier from the Battle of White Plains reportedly died in the early hours of November 1, 1776. "Was it fate that the Hessian's last night among the living was All Hallows' Eve? Surely no ghost in all the world could ask for a finer birthday," he continued.

Historic photo of the Headless Horseman Bridge that replaced the original wooden bridge. *Photo courtesy of the Detroit Publishing Company.*

While Rondina was determined to find the name for the headless ghost, author Edgar Mayhew Bacon reported in his *Chronicles of Tarrytown and Sleepy Hollow* several firsthand accounts of a fearless phantom haunting what was the village of North Tarrytown in the late 1800s.

One story involved an Irishwoman who spotted a headless specter on horseback near the Old Dutch Church in the 1870s. "There was no doubting the sincerity of the ghost-seer," Bacon wrote. "Had she possibly had her imagination fired by reading Irving? It was easier to believe that she had seen the headless Hessian."

Bacon told another story of a man who made the trek over the Headless Horseman Bridge late one night on his way home from a local tavern. "He was dragged upon the bridge by invisible hands, though it was clear moonlight, and flung over the high parapet into the water of the Pocantico, where he swam for some time," he wrote, adding that there was another account of a man who was attacked by an unseen force and somehow avoided being thrown over the bridge.

Bacon's book was originally published in 1897, and these three accounts seem to have taken place decades after Irving penned the original tale.

Have locals spotted the phantom rider recently? Yes, according to *Hudson Valley* magazine: "Rumors of Headless Horseman sightings surge amid visits to Philipsburg Manor and Irving's Sunnyside home," wrote Sabrina Sucator in the October 15, 2021 edition of the publication.

It shouldn't be a surprise, but the magazine article reported that paranormal activity seems to amp up around Halloween.

IRVING'S GHOSTS

Based purely on the various supernatural themes and spooky lore explored in the celebrated writer's body of work, there's no denying that he lived a haunted life.

But what came first, Washington Irving's terrifying tales or the ghosts that inspired him?

Alex Matsuo, author of *Women of the Paranormal* and content creator with the *Spooky Stuff* blog, believes Irving's stories had the potential to create what paranormal researchers call "egregores," or a nonphysical entity or thought-form manifestation that can arise from the collective thoughts and emotions of a group of people.

"There is a lot of history surrounding the area with some pivotal moments that contributed to the establishment of the United States," Matsuo told me. "There's also a lot of Indigenous history that was buried by the victors, usually white Europeans, who inadvertently tried to change the narrative of history."

If a ghost is history demanding to be remembered, Matsuo said there is likely a combination of residual energy lingering in the shadows of Sleepy Hollow coupled with actual hauntings that may have been amplified—or even created—by Irving's stories.

"When it comes to the paranormal activity in the area, there's a lot to unpack and it has multiple layers between hauntings caused by people, controversy and politics," Matsuo said. "I would be really interested in seeing what the activity was like before and after Irving's story became famous as well as that 'in-between time' before Tarrytown and Sleepy Hollow got a resurgence in popularity."

While Irving became an international sensation with the release of *The Sketch Book*, which was written over the winter of 1819 and 1820 and penned while Irving was in England, a majority of the author's tales after "The Legend of Sleepy Hollow" had a paranormal theme. In fact, nearly forty out of sixty-one stories he wrote had some supernatural elements.

Based on the concept of manifesting thought-forms and the popularity of Irving's work, the idea that his imagination somehow created a few of the specters of the Hudson Valley region is a viable possibility.

There's also the notion that Irving merely chronicled the tales of preexisting ghosts. In fact, many of the characters in "The Legend of Sleepy Hollow" and his nonfiction sequel of sorts, "A Chronicle of Wolfert's Roost," were loosely based on actual people and lore.

He did, however, take some creative liberties.

Matsuo wrote about the real people who inspired Irving's famous tale in her *Spooky Stuff* blog. Ichabod Crane, for example, was indeed a person, and "Irving saw his name in a paper and really liked it," Matsuo wrote. "The real Crane served during the War of 1812 and was alive at the same time as Washington Irving. However, the two never met. Crane was a military man and served for 45 years. What's funny is that he wasn't exactly thrilled about Irving using his real name in the story. He's also the exact opposite of the fictional Crane."

Postcard of Washington Irving's Sunnyside printed by the Albertype Company. *Courtesy of Card Cow.*

Two schoolteachers, Samuel Youngs and Jesse Merwin, served as the actual inspiration for the easily spooked Crane. "Youngs and Irving were actually pretty close friends," Matsuo penned. "He was honestly delighted to be the inspiration for Ichabod. He's buried at the Old Dutch Church in Sleepy Hollow. The other person who was believed to be Ichabod's inspiration is Jesse Merwin, who was a teacher in Kinderhook, NY. The one-room schoolhouse he taught in still stands today and you can see it in person."

According to Matsuo's blog post, the Van Tassels and Brom Bones were real people too. "Irving's sister boarded at the Van Tassel home and they were neighbors," Matsuo reported. "He reimagined the Val Tassels as a wealthy family. Eleanor Van Tassel Brush is likely to be the inspiration for Katrina Van Tassel. The name Katrina likely came from Eleanor's aunt, Catrina."

Sleepy Hollow's alpha male rabble-rouser was loosely based on Abraham Martling, nicknamed Brom. "He was the town blacksmith and he rode a giant black horse, much like the Headless Horseman in the story," Matsuo noted.

In Irving's "A Chronicle of Wolfert's Roost," he explored the legends, ghost stories and superstitions surrounding the Van Tassel farmhouse, a property the famed writer purchased when he returned from Europe. Irving made extensive renovations to the home and renamed it Sunnyside.

The story explored how the spellbound region was supposedly cursed by a Native American sachem and was once home to a witch. He even discussed the Van Tassel family's backstory during the American Revolution.

Irving also wrote about his face-to-face encounter with a female spirit in "Wolfert's Roost," an apparition he saw only once. "There is one room in the mansion which almost overhangs the river, and is reputed to be haunted by the ghost of a young lady who died of love and green apples," he penned.

The story was passed down by family members after the author's passing and was even discussed in the October 5, 1947 edition of the *New York Times*. The piece, "Irving's Home Opens with Two Ghosts," talked about the property's public grand opening thanks to financial support from the Rockefeller family.

While the brokenhearted female spirit has rarely been mentioned since Sunnyside reopened as a museum, Matsuo red-flagged Irving's narrative about the lovelorn resident ghost.

"I have mixed thoughts because it's always a woman with some sort of unfinished business," Matsuo said. "You don't hear a lot of stories about a wailing man or a gentleman looking for his lost love. Sometimes it makes me

Washington Irving's gravestone located in Sleepy Hollow Cemetery. *Photo courtesy of Lee Snider from Depositphotos.*

wonder if it's because the man was able to cross over because he was more intelligent and well to do, while the woman is completely lost without him."

Matsuo added that she has been researching stories with gendered undertones and believes "it's much more complex than what is on the surface."

Irving never mentioned if the mystery ghost actually died from ingesting green apples or simply had an affinity for them. In folklore, there's a magical connotation to the forbidden fruit, suggesting that there may have been some sort of witchery involved. His ambiguous description of the experience may be more telling about the writer's views of women and less about the supposed ghostly activity.

With that being said, the spirit is significant because her apparition is among the few Irving actually witnessed himself while living at his allegedly haunted home overlooking the Hudson River.

For the record, the spirit was relocated from the upstairs bedroom to outside in the orchard based on Irving's great-great-grandnephew's retelling of the story in the 1940s. Apparently, she got a downgrade in the afterlife. How 'bout them apples?

MATILDA HOFFMAN

The enchanted land surrounding Washington Irving's Sunnyside is apparently a hotbed of paranormal activity. In addition to the young lady who died of love and green apples, there's another spirit rumored to wander among the dense thicket and labyrinthine paths outside of the famed writer's later-in-life home.

Her name? Matilda Hoffman.

"Irving's shy and beguiling fiancée is said to haunt a trove of trees from which she watches Irving's cottage," reported Jerry Eimbinder in the September 30, 2011 edition of *Tarrytown–Sleepy Hollow Patch*. "She died on April 26, 1809 at the age of seventeen from complications from a cold that led to consumption."

Leanna Renee Hieber, coauthor of *A Haunted History of Invisible Women*, told me that it seems a bit farfetched to think that Hoffman's spirit made the trek from Manhattan to the Hudson Valley to keep a postmortem watch over Irving's home.

"I'm inclined to think this is more a lovelorn projection continuing the ghost story tropes of tragic romance as part of storytelling allure," Hieber

Matilda Hoffman is said to be one of the spirits haunting Sunnyside in Tarrytown, New York. *Courtesy of Card Cow.*

said. "The fact that Irving never married, though he did try to court others, adds to the idea that Matilda was his one true love. But in life she wouldn't have had a tie to that particular house."

Hieber said she's heard about similar love stories that transcend death while giving tours with NYC's Boroughs of the Dead. But she reiterated that Irving had a history of blurring fact and fiction by controlling the narrative of his life story.

"A ghost might, on a rare occasion, 'move' with a loved one to a new place," she explained. "In that case it is tied more to the living than to buildings known to them in life, but I think this is more people wanting to believe in a connection," she said. "It could very well be another unnamed woman of history instead, passing through that property."

What really happened between the young couple that possibly left such an indelible mark?

Hieber said that Irving's health was fragile in his youth, which is "one of the reasons he was permitted more leniency in the family than his elder brothers, who sent him abroad to study in Europe and recover there."

Irving's short courtship with Hoffman appeared to be more of a May-September romance than a tragic, Shakespearean love story. "Upon his return to New York, Irving began studying law with his mentor Judge Josiah

Ogden Hoffman. Enamored with the judge's daughter Matilda, theirs was an organic meeting and courtship," Hieber explained. "Irving and Matilda were engaged by the time she contracted tuberculosis and she died at the tender age of seventeen."

While the not-yet-famous writer was obviously heartbroken over Hoffman's painful death. Hieber told me that Irving didn't write much about the loss of his fiancée. "There's one faintly penciled diary line noting Matilda's passing, and it isn't known whether their relationship and losing her directly inspired some of his writing or whether that's reader projection," she said. "It is known he was deeply distraught after her passing in 1809, the emotional toll delayed his publication of his *History of New-York*, the book that would truly put him on the map."

While it's highly unlikely that Hoffman is haunting a trove of trees outside of Irving's Sunnyside, there is a possibility that her ghost is still lingering in the afterlife at her final resting spot in New York City's east side.

She's buried in the cemetery outside of the historic St. Mark's Church-in-the-Bowery. There are reports of a woman fitting her description, wearing period garb and sitting in the pews in the house of worship that was completed and consecrated on May 9, 1799. When visitors to the church approach the female apparition, she disappears.

Could it be Hoffman? Hieber isn't convinced.

"It's hard to pin this figure down because this church has a longer history than nearly any other structure left in the city; only St. Paul's Chapel downtown shares a comparably storied history as the oldest church still standing in Manhattan," Hieber told me. "It's true that whenever there is death, loss and a romantic connection, especially tied to a young woman, it leads the living to want to ascribe hauntings to her. Especially considering we're still telling Irving's stories, in some ways he keeps her alive by his own cultural influence on the city."

The coauthor of *A Haunted History of Invisible Women* cited a quote from Edgar Allan Poe, who lost his beloved wife, Virginia, to the same disease. "The death of a beautiful woman is, unquestionably, the most poetical topic in the world," he lamented.

Hieber said that Poe isn't romanticizing death in his famous quote. "He's grappling with it in his own life as a prompt for writing," she said. "I think that sense of wanting to preserve the mysterious beauty of a life cut short continues to drive ghost stories."

With that being said, Hieber isn't completely ruling out the possibility that Hoffman's spirit may be hanging out in the pews of one of New York

Washington Irving's beloved Matilda Hoffman is buried in the churchyard of Manhattan's St. Mark's Church-in-the-Bowery. *Photo by Sam Baltrusis.*

City's oldest holy haunts. "While it could be any period penitent in those pews, because we know more about Matilda than the average woman of the congregation and due to her burial on the grounds, her connection to the site has credence," Hieber added.

In addition to the female spirit haunting St. Mark's Church-in-the-Bowery, the original owner of the land, Peter Stuyvesant, is interred in a vault under the chapel. Nicknamed the "peg-leg Dutchman" after losing his appendage on an adventure in Curaçao, Stuyvesant's spirit supposedly walks with a cane and has been disrupting church services for centuries according to the *NYC Ghosts* website.

"Stuyvesant, undeniably the church's paranormal patriarch, likes to join in on all the creativity," reported *NYC Ghosts*. "He is known for chiming in on hymns in his native tongue, for instance. In 1930, he was seen sitting among congregation members. When the bells at St. Mark's Church rang on their own in 1965, people also believed it was him."

Foreman Cole, who was hired by the congregation to wind its clock, has reportedly spotted a female apparition more than a dozen times standing on the balcony and wearing a wide skirt.

The late Hans Holzier interviewed Cole in his book *This House Is Haunted*. The NYC-based paranormal investigator asked Cole if there was anything peculiar about his encounter with the female spirit haunting the church. His response: "Yes, there was. She seemed to ignore me, looked right through me, and did not respond to my words."

Holzer did bring in one of his medium friends, Mary R.M., to help him investigate the property. While she was able to pinpoint the male spirit who walked with a cane as Stuyvesant, the psychic was a bit ambiguous with her take on the female energy haunting the house of worship.

According to Holzer, his friend saw a woman wearing period garb near the back door of the church. "I see a white shape floating away from that marble slab in the rear," Mary told Holzer.

Could this be the residual haunting of the author's beloved Matilda? Perhaps. It's important to note that Irving's spirit has been seen at the Public Theatre, which had a past life as the Astor Library. St. Mark's Church is only a few blocks away from the famed writer's former stomping grounds on Lafayette Street in Manhattan.

Because of the proximity of the two haunts, it would make sense if Irving and Hoffman continued their courtship among the pews of the historic church in NYC followed by a postmortem move to Irving's beloved Sunnyside.

Love from beyond the grave? Anything is possible.

SUNNYSIDE'S SPIRITS

Out of all of the ghosts supposedly haunting Washington Irving's Sunnyside, the one who makes the most sense is "The Legend of Sleepy Hollow" author himself.

According to several reports, Irving's spirit sticks around his former home.

The same *Patch* article that claimed the ghosts of Matilda Hoffman and the lady who died of love and green apples roam the property also noted that "the first American writer to gain old-world respect and recognition for the new-world's literature" continues to linger inside Sunnyside.

"He experienced periods of gloom and obsession with death during his lifetime," wrote Jerry Eimbinder in the *Tarrytown–Sleepy Hollow Patch*. "His ghost has been reportedly seen in a window of a bedroom that faces the Hudson River and also in his study located on the east side of the cottage, away from the river."

Leanna Renee Hieber, coauthor of *A Haunted History of Invisible Women*, told me that writers tend to leave a psychic imprint at the locations where they created their stories. "It's very common for hauntings to circulate around a public figure's home, particularly authors and especially if their work had any supernatural or ghostly elements to them," Hieber said. "I think folks expect an author to haunt the places where they wrote."

The 1885 bust of Washington Irving, who never actually lived on Irving Place in New York City, is by Friedrich Beer. *Photo by Sam Baltrusis.*

As someone who also writes spooky stories, Hieber told me that she has "left a bit of a psychic and energetic imprint on the places where I've consistently written and created emotionally impactful tales."

Hieber explained that writing paranormal-themed material can amplify the residual energy where the work is created. "Writing about ghosts in both a fiction and nonfiction capacity, I can confirm that the process feels like channeling; much like a Spiritualist would describe mediumship," she said. "I think that the creative space is a spiritual one and I think that because the living are still reading Irving and telling his stories, we're still summoning him."

Irving died in his upstairs bedroom on November 28, 1859, from a heart attack. He was seventy-six years old. According to legend, his last words were: "Well, I must arrange my pillows for another night. When will this end?"

In 1843, Irving wrote, "I really believe that when I die I shall haunt it [Sunnyside]; but it will be as a good spirit, that no one needs to be afraid of." He wanted to be an "amiable ghost," and based on several reports, his wishes came true.

"A few years after his death, three people watched as Irving's spirit walked through the parlor of Sunnyside, disappearing into the library," wrote Cheri Farnsworth in *Haunted Hudson Valley*. "Washington Irving obviously loved a good ghost story, and it was no secret how much he loved his Sunnyside estate. By haunting Sunnyside, he could enjoy both."

When Irving moved into the two-bedroom stone cottage in 1835, the famed writer was intrigued by reports of the previous owner, Wolfert Acker, haunting the apple orchard. And of course, Irving briefly witnessed the apparition of a young lady who died of love and green apples in the building's upstairs bedroom as he recalled in his nonfiction piece "A Chronicle of Wolfert's Roost."

But wait, there's more. Another story involved Abraham Lincoln's funeral train, which makes a yearly pilgrimage in April. According to the legend, a fourteen-car train led by a black locomotive sets off its whistle as it approaches Sunnyside.

"The piercing sound wakes Irving's ghost as the train chugs toward Tarrytown carrying Abraham Lincoln's body, just as his funeral train did in 1865 when it traveled from New York City to Buffalo and eventually to Springfield, Ohio, [*sic*] Lincoln's final burying place," reported the *Tarrytown–Sleepy Hollow Patch*.

The article also mentioned that Irving's five nieces still stick around in the afterlife. "They were the daughters of Irving's elder brother Ebenezer," Eimbinder wrote. "After the visitors are gone, they still tidy the house."

Why all of this alleged paranormal activity at Sunnyside? My friend Dana Boadway, who happens to be a high-priestess witch, believes it's the cottage's close proximity to the Hudson River coupled with the train tracks on the shoreline of the writer's property.

"They both flow from place to place in constant motion, making a pathway through the earth," Boadway told me. "Humans replicate the way water changes the landforms with the construction of train tracks. When you think about the sheer power of water being able to carve through solid rock, and the constant movement, it makes sense," she said, adding that the original trains were powered by water. "Humans have learned how to

The ghost of Washington Irving has been spotted from the window of the author's upstairs bedroom. *Photo by Sam Baltrusis.*

harness that energy to power whole cities and spirits can somehow tap into that energy to become stronger."

In other words, the water and the train tracks somehow amplify the paranormal activity at Sunnyside and serve as a postmortem power station.

It should be no surprise that researchers have noted a correlation between sources of water, train tracks and residual hauntings. Back in 2012 when I interviewed Michael Baker, the founder of the science-based research group called the New England Center for the Advancement of the Paranormal Science or NECAPS, he told me that patterns emerged when his group created a database of reports collected from various haunted locations.

Based on his group's data-mining project, there were two themes that emerged at locales with higher incidents of ghostly activity. The two factors? Trains and water.

While there has been very little chatter about the motley crew of spirits haunting the property since the cottage became a museum, there was one recent report of a young visitor who snapped a photograph from outside of the house.

Rachel Lambert, a teen from Rotterdam, visited Sunnyside on June 26, 2010. While taking a tour of the property, the young paranormal enthusiast snapped a picture after seeing something strange in one of the upstairs windows.

What Lambert spotted in the image the following day was shocking. "She and her family were able to make out a figure that looks like the head and upper body of a ghost holding a quill pen," reported Madeleine Dopico in the *Tarrytown–Sleepy Hollow Patch*. "Rachel determined that before her eyes was a picture of the ghost of Washington Irving."

While the spokesperson from Historic Hudson Valley told the community journalist that he was "unaware" of any ghosts at the estate, a paranormal investigator from Haunted Hudson Valley validated Lambert's spirit photo.

"The legend says he still haunts the house," said Donna Davies. "If he was going to haunt any place, he would haunt Sunnyside."

The article also pointed out the poetic justice of the situation: America's most beloved ghost story writer passed away in his home and then stuck around in the afterlife? Yes, even Diedrich Knickerbocker himself couldn't have staged a more fitting last hurrah.

CHAPTER 3
THE GHOSTS

When master storyteller Jonathan Kruk performed his spirited rendition of Washington Irving's "The Legend of Sleepy Hollow" at Sunnyside on Halloween, the veil between the living and dead oddly lifted.

It was a magical night.

"I do feel the spirits around me," he said during a sit-down interview months after his performance on All Hallows' Eve. "I've done the story so many times, it has become a part of me. I always invoke Washington Irving's protective spirit just to calm myself down. As I amble down the walkway at Sunnyside, I say a little prayer to his spirit to fill my voice with the same inspiration he had when he wrote the tale. But it's mostly about asking for stamina. I perform 'The Legend of Sleepy Hollow' at least fifty times every season and it can be exhausting."

While Kruk told me that several audience members insisted that he was sharing the stage with spirits during his performances over the years, the author of *Legends and Lore of Sleepy Hollow and the Hudson Valley* said he's never seen an apparition manifest in front of him at Sunnyside.

He does, however, feel haunted by spirits.

"It's not a typical ghost where it appears and gallops into my dreams," he explained. "The story is so embedded in my consciousness that I'm literally begging the spirit of Irving to give me the inspiration and voice to perform his story once again."

Master storyteller
Jonathan Kruk's
interpretation of
"The Legend of
Sleepy Hollow"
has become
a Halloween
tradition in the
Hudson Valley.
*Photo by Rudolf Von
Dommele.*

Kruk said he does notice a shift of energy in Sleepy Hollow during the month of October. But is it haunted? Yes, he told me, but not in the way that it's often portrayed on-screen.

"It's such a beautiful, pastoral location," he said. "Telling the story not only invokes the spirits of the Headless Horseman or Major André or the wailing women in white, but the whole region as Irving said is abounding with ghosts. Whether it's the crisp spirit of autumn or an actual diabolical ghost without a head, there's an enchantment throughout the entire area. It's as if you're thrust back in time and into another century. There's something in the trees and in the Hudson River that almost seems supernatural."

Kruk shifted in and out of various characters throughout the interview. For example, when he talked about the time a retired NYC police officer swore he captured a ghost with Kruk in a photograph, the actor's voice transformed into a thick Brooklyn accent.

"He was convinced there was a ghost standing right behind me," Kruk recalled. "I have to accept that even though I haven't had Irving's ghost put an icy hand on my shoulder and whisper in my ear that he's with me while I perform, I know in my heart it's true."

While Kruk hasn't seen a ghost during a performance, he did have a firsthand experience more than two decades ago in the Sparta Cemetery in nearby Ossining, New York.

"I was looking for the grave of a popular figure in local lore known as the Leatherman. It was around twilight on a summer day and I just couldn't find his grave marker. I was on top of the hill looking down and I saw what appeared to be a young woman with an Empire-style white dress and a parasol," he recalled. "At first I thought she was a fellow performer or a reenactor from Philipsburg Manor walking through the cemetery. I noticed her below the crest of a domed hill and I thought I would come around to the other side and ask her if she knew where the Leatherman's grave was located. As I approached her, she disappeared into thin air."

Kruk said he was frightened by the ghost at first and ran back to his car for a quick escape. While he was searching for his keys, he felt something inexplicable next to him in the passenger seat. "I felt a presence to my right and thought to myself that I was going to see something straight out of a gory horror film," he said. "I turned, and instead of finding an apparition to my right, I found the tombstone of the Leatherman. I somehow parked my vehicle right next to it."

For the record, the Leatherman was a mysterious figure in local lore who was famous for wearing his handmade leather suits as he traveled through the Northeast on a journey between the Connecticut River and the Hudson River from roughly 1857 to 1889.

Kruk said the legendary man's original gravesite was only a few feet from the highway at the time, so his remains were exhumed and reburied inside the Sparta Cemetery with a new marker in 2011.

As the go-to expert on the Hudson Valley's lore, Kruk told me he didn't necessarily start his career with an interest in Irving's stories, but they have somehow become his passion. "It wasn't something I aspired to do when I was in college," he said. "I first began telling a shorter version of the story in 1996 for Historic Hudson Valley. There were only a couple of weekend events, but it was extremely popular. So they revamped everything in 2010 and teamed me up with musician Jim Keyes. Historic Hudson Valley then put us in the Old Dutch Church, and that began our performances of 'The Legend of Sleepy Hollow,' which eventually moved to Sunnyside."

Has the master storyteller uncovered any reliable reports of the Headless Horseman over the years?

Kruk said that a few of the tourists who visit Sleepy Hollow during October seem to almost "conjure up ghosts in their imaginations," but he has heard at least one credible encounter from a local. "The only story of what could be a Headless Horseman sighting came from a chef at the Sleepy

Altar at the Old Dutch Church built in 1685 and the original home of Jonathan Kruk's performances of "The Legend of Sleepy Hollow." *Photo courtesy of Lee Snider from Depositphotos.*

Hollow Country Club," Kruk said. "He spotted the Headless Horseman in more of an auditory and olfactory sort of way, but the spirit was completely invisible to him."

The author said the lack of actual Headless Horseman sightings may be related to Irving's ambiguity in the original tale. While Kruk believes the origin story of the ghostly rider was inspired by a composite of several men who lost their heads during the American Revolution, he thinks there was a more realistic explanation to the fictional phantom.

"I believe it was Brom Bones dressed up as the Headless Horseman," Kruk told me. "Based on my research, there was a custom at the time to frighten off people who weren't sincere about becoming part of the community."

While Kruk said Irving's headless Hessian has gotten more sinister in the way he's portrayed in pop culture, the master storyteller told me that he has become more open to the paranormal since his first encounter at Sparta Cemetery more than twenty years ago. "Not all spirits have to be malevolent," he said. "Irving himself actually said that he would pleasantly haunt Sunnyside as 'an amicable ghost,' and I do feel deep down that he does."

BRONZE LADY

If there is a ghostly legend that could rival the popularity of Washington Irving's galloping ghoul, it would be the Bronze Lady who sits atop a hill deep inside the Sleepy Hollow Cemetery.

The statue, a larger-than-life woman cast in metal, is a stone's throw from the re-created Headless Horseman Bridge. Her back is turned to the breathtaking view of the Hudson River, and two small trees are growing on either side of the eerie sculpture, which feels like a doorway to another realm.

There's an inexplicable energy emanating from the Bronze Lady as she keeps watch of her husband's crypt positioned directly across from her forlorn, downward gaze. She's cursed, according to local legend, and anyone who dares cross her threshold in the wee hours of the night and disrespects her will pay the ultimate price.

Hell hath no fury like the Bronze Lady scorned.

Emily Faber, a journalist with Sinclair Broadcast group, reported on October 20, 2021, of "a bronze woman who gazes at the tomb of a Civil War general and has been heard crying." Faber wrote, "Some brave enough to approach the statue have described feeling real tears beneath her eyes. Others have experienced bouts of bad luck after touching the statue's face in an irreverent way."

Anthony J. Marmo, a Tarrytown native, recalled how it was a rite of passage to visit the Bronze Lady in Sleepy Hollow Cemetery. "If you knocked on the door of the general's tomb and looked through the keyhole, you would have a bad dream that night. Of course, that always worked. There was another one where, if you slapped her in the face, sat in her lap and spit in her eye, she would haunt you for the rest of your life. There was always one brave kid who did it," Marmo said in an interview in the October 29, 2000 edition of the *New York Times*.

"When we got older, we'd be the ones bringing new kids up," Marmo remembered from his childhood in the 1970s. "One of us would hide behind the statue and come out screaming if a kid had the nerve to sit in her lap—terrorize him, you know."

Jeannie Galgano told the *New York Times* reporter Robyn Leary that she dared to approach the Bronze Lady in the 1960s. "When we were kids, the deal was that you were brave if you went up to the Bronze Lady and you sat in her lap and slapped her across the face and kicked her in the shins," Galgano said. "Then you had to go across to the door of the mausoleum

According to urban legend, the Bronze Lady will inflict a curse if she is disrespected. *Photo by Angela Artuso.*

and knock on it three times—and if you did all that, she would come and haunt you. We did it a couple of times but she never came to haunt us."

The statue was commissioned by Ann Thomas, the widow of a Civil War general who passed away in 1903. Andrew O'Connor, a prominent sculptor

The Bronze Lady sits atop a hill overlooking the crypt of a Civil War general. *Photo by Angela Artuso.*

of the time, created the piece, called *Recueillement, or Grief.* The widow was unhappy with the finished statue, and Thomas requested a happier face gazing at her husband's mausoleum.

O'Connor cast a less melancholic head. But as soon as the widow told him she liked it, he smashed it on the floor, telling her: "I just made this to show you that I could do it. I should never let such a monstrosity out of my studio."

After Thomas passed in 1944, she was interred next to her husband. In the following years, the Bronze Lady earned urban legend status, and the statue's supernatural powers became more elaborate. If locals crossed her the wrong way, they could be cursed for life.

Alex Matsuo, an author who has written about Sleepy Hollow Cemetery in her *Spooky Stuff* blog, thought the Bronze Lady lore was a bit over the top until she had an odd encounter with the statue during an afternoon visit.

"I really wanted to see the Bronze Lady because the backstory behind it and the urban legends that developed since were fascinating to me," Matsuo told me. "As I was trying to take pictures and videos, my camera kept glitching. Some videos even had a really weird shaking to it even though my hand was completely still. Whenever I took video, it would freeze and almost act like an old computer from the early 1990s. It was very bizarre."

Matsuo didn't want to poke the bear, so she quickly made amends.

"Just to make sure I had all my bases covered, I apologized to the Bronze Lady for taking her photo without her permission," she said. "After I said my apology and asked if I could take some photos and video so I could tell her story."

No surprise, but after Matsuo apologized to the Bronze Lady, she said, "the quality went back to normal."

As far as ghost lore associated with the statue, one story is if you sit on the Bronze Lady's lap and then peek into the keyhole in the door of the crypt, you'll see a ghost. It's said that the statue has actually animated, as if it had come to life, and then proceeded to sob uncontrollably. Tears, and even blood, have been spotted streaming from her downturned eyes.

According to Faber's article, the Bronze Lady isn't the only ghost haunting the Sleepy Hollow Cemetery. One investigator reportedly picked up the sound of musket gunfire and a drum line from a section of the cemetery where several Revolutionary War soldiers are buried. There was another weird story involving a large shadow entity with the face of a raccoon lurking in the shadows.

The Bronze Lady, however, continues to be the main attraction for thrill-seekers looking for a ghostly encounter. As far as the supposed curse, all of the locals interviewed for the *New York Times* article seemed to avoid the enchanted statue's wrath except for one woman who tempted fate in the 1970s.

"I scoffed at the tale," Emily Storms Arminio confessed to Leary. "But two days after I touched the Bronze Lady's face, a storm brought down a tree limb that crushed my Camaro."

CAPTAIN KIDD

The ghost of the infamous privateer Captain William Kidd apparently gets around. The rabble-rouser was originally from across the pond in Scotland but relocated to Manhattan as a young man.

He was commissioned by Richard Coote, the governor of New York, Massachusetts Bay and New Hampshire, in 1695 to hunt down pirates in the Indian Ocean. The tides quickly turned for Kidd after he failed to track down many of the enemy vessels, and after threats of mutiny from his crew, he was arrested and executed.

The English quickly turned their collective back on Kidd because he apparently opted for the Jolly Roger flag over the Union Jack.

His legend flourished after he was hanged in an extremely crude torture device known as a gibbet cage in 1701. His rogue life on the high seas became fodder for several pirate-themed books that hinted at the possibility that Kidd may have hidden his stolen stash.

His spirit allegedly haunts several locations on the East Coast, including a historic cemetery in Boston, Massachusetts. Why the Bay State? "Boston is where he was arrested on charges of murder and piracy. He was imprisoned there until he was transported to London to stand trial," said Cindy Vallar, editor of the *Pirates and Privateers* newsletter.

Kidd's ghost is rumored to linger next to an unmarked grave at the rear of King's Chapel Burying Ground on Tremont Street. People claim to hear the raucous laughter of a pirate echoing throughout the cemetery. Although the gravestone has no name, the legend is it's Kidd's final resting place.

Captain William Kidd in New York Harbor by J.L.G. Ferris was published in the Foundation Press in 1932. *Courtesy of the Library of Congress.*

According to Vallar, it's not. While the salty dog was definitely arrested in Boston in 1701 and was hanged and buried in England, little proof exists to either support or disprove the idea that he haunts the historic burying ground.

Vallar told me revisionism is commonplace when it comes to pirates. "I think word of mouth plays a key role. It's kind of like the whisper down the lane. One person tells the story, but the next tweaks it, and the teller after that does the same until the original version and the revised version no longer resemble each other. It's what makes good storytelling."

Speaking of historical inaccuracies associated with pirate lore, there's another legend implying that Kidd's spirit lingers near a rock formation facing the Hudson River in Tarrytown.

"Captain Kidd is said to have buried his treasure in locations between the coast of Maine and the Florida Keys, including places along the Hudson River," wrote Ellen McHale in the *Hudson Valley Viewfinder* magazine. "In many tales, Captain Kidd—who was executed for murder and piracy—is the ghostly protector of his treasure. When two soldiers commenced digging at one purported hiding place along the Hudson in 1825, the story goes that a menacing figure rose from the ground and caused the men to faint. Both swore it was the specter of Kidd, keeping watch over his loot."

One of the haunted hot spots known as "Kidd's Rock" is located in Kingsland Point, a waterfront area in Sleepy Hollow near the Lyndhurst estate. "Legend has it this massive boulder was a meeting place for Frederick Philipse, lord of a 52,000-acre manor on the shores of the Hudson River, and the notorious pirate Captain Kidd," wrote Jim Logan in the *Sleepy Hollow Country* blog. "Piracy would have been a huge issue for Philipse, whose trade depended on sea routes between the Caribbean, New York, and Europe. This alleged rendezvous is in fairly close proximity to Philipsburg Manor, Philipse's northernmost trading center and the location of his grist mill."

Edward Mayhew Bacon explored the rumors of buried treasure in his book *Chronicles of Tarrytown and Sleepy Hollow*. "This has long been the name of a rock that is part of the river-wall on the outer side of Kingsland's point," Bacon wrote. "There is a summer-house built over the

Captain Kidd hanging in chains.

Captain Kidd hanging in a gibbet cage as depicted in an illustration from the Marine Research Society published in 1924. *Courtesy of the Library of Congress.*

rock and if there were ever golden riches beneath it, or if there are treasures hidden there still, it is not the duty of a sober historian to tell."

The legend also suggested that several faithful pirates from Kidd's ship, *Adventure Galley*, guarded the old salt's booty in the afterlife. "When Captain Kidd buried gold and other loot, his crew members drew lots," reported Jerry Eimbinder in the September 30, 2011 edition of *Tarrytown–Sleepy Hollow Patch*. "The losers were killed and their bodies were placed on top of the treasure chests to repel intruders. As ghosts, they remain fierce sentries destined to guard Kidd's treasures forever."

In addition to the pirate posse protecting their plundered goods in the Hudson Valley, one of the men Kidd reportedly killed haunts the area too. However, he wasn't part of the suicide ghost pact. The unwilling victim was allegedly hit over the head with an iron water bucket, and he supposedly seeks postmortem revenge.

There's also a ghostly woman lingering around Tarrytown's waterfront who was mistaken as Kidd's bride, according to Eimbinder. "She was captured in Tarrytown, tried for piracy and executed. She is believed to be either a traveler who booked passage to Tarrytown looking for work or a slave or servant intended for a rich merchant. Her ghost proclaims her innocence as she waits for the vessel that brought her to Tarrytown believing it is coming to her rescue," he wrote in the *Patch* article.

Sleepy Hollow wasn't his only haunted hideout in New York. The captain allegedly hid gold and other bounty throughout the Hudson River Valley, including "Money Hill at Croton Point, on the summit of Crow Nest mountain, near Kidd's Cove in the town of Esopus, and even as far inland as the Catskill Mountains," Logan penned in his "Captain Kidd's Rock" article. "Some legends even repeat that Captain Kidd scuttled his treasure ship off Jones Point at the foot of Dunderberg Mountain."

Haunted pirate treasure? Shiver me timbers.

HULDA THE WITCH

The story of Hulda, a Bohemian immigrant who was supposedly vilified by the tight-knit Sleepy Hollow community for being a witch, has evolved over the years.

Some believe she's the German that Washington Irving referenced in "The Legend of Sleepy Hollow" as having bewitched the area so that a "drowsy, dreamy influence seems to hang over the land." She even has been credited with standing up to the British when they charged the town in 1777.

According to the legend, Hulda showed up with her musket in hand to fight for the community that shunned her and was ultimately killed in the skirmish. She allegedly died behind the Old Dutch Church, near the marker honoring her in the burial ground.

The gravestone, which was crafted to look like a winged-soul effigy from the 1700s, was actually erected in 2019 and honors this brave woman who supposedly died for her country.

The issue? Historians aren't convinced that Hulda from Bohemia ever existed.

J.W. Ocker, author of *The New York Grimpendium*, told me that Hulda has become a big draw for Sleepy Hollow over the past few years. But he's concerned that Hulda has been presented almost as a martyred superhero even though it's likely that her backstory was an old wives' tale that has been twisted over time.

A sandstone grave marker was created in 2019 in honor of the fictional Hulda the Witch in the Old Dutch Burying Ground. *Photo by Angela Artuso.*

"Suddenly locals now have their own witch, even though it's probably a completely fictitious story," Ocker told me. "Not only have they grabbed onto her, associated a gravestone to her in the Old Dutch Burying Ground, but they turned her into Xena the Warrior Princess. Somehow, she single-handedly won the American Revolution and was this feminist icon. It's completely not true."

Jim Logan, the superintendent of Sleepy Hollow Cemetery, penned a persuasive argument that Hulda was never meant to be more than a legend that was first told by Edgar Mayhew Bacon in his 1897 book *Chronicles of Tarrytown and Sleepy Hollow*.

"Hulda the witch of Sleepy Hollow has over the last decade performed a most difficult feat: she has transformed from a minor fictional character into a real person, complete with a headstone in a place of honor at a local church," Logan wrote on the website *Sleepy Hollow Country*. "Bacon clearly intends the reader to understand that maybe once, long ago, a person like Hulda may have been rooted in some semblance of truth. Or perhaps not. Hulda the witch, in Bacon's telling, is clearly a myth."

According to Bacon's original tale, Hulda lived in a cottage in the woods and was known to deliver baskets of herbal remedies and provisions to families hit hard during the American Revolution. Because of her witchy reputation in the village, the locals would turn her gifts away. When the community was besieged by the British, Bacon said she picked up her rifle and fought to protect her land and was tragically killed by the redcoats.

"Animated by a new respect, those who had seen her fight avowed that, witch or no witch, she had earned a right to a Christian burial," Bacon wrote, adding that the locals found a Bible in her cabin in the woods along with a note willing her gold to the widows whose husbands had fallen for their country.

While Bacon's tale seemed farfetched at the time, several contemporary authors and journalists embellished her legend even more by claiming she traded with the Native Americans and spoke several languages. She was even presented as a fearless patriot in an article in the November 28, 1975 edition of the *Tarrytown Daily News*.

In the write-up, a man named "Old Ben" supposedly witnessed Hulda die for her country in a battle that never actually happened outside of the Old Dutch Church. "Things looked really bad. The redcoats out-numbered us three to one. We were getting the worst of it," the article claimed. "About this time, Hulda appeared, carrying her musket. She took a place in the front line. She fought better than a dozen of us. She renewed our courage. On that day, Hulda the witch turned the tide for us."

In a town famous for its legends and lore, it should be no surprise that Sleepy Hollow's official witch is completely fabricated. But what's the underlying motive behind Hulda's made-up narrative? According to authors Alex Matsuo and Leanna Renee Hieber, it's a complicated myth to untangle.

Matsuo, author of *Women of the Paranormal*, told me that even though Hulda may have been a fictional character, her story is emblematic of an issue outsiders have faced for centuries. "Vilification within a community is complicated because it's rarely what it is at surface level," Matsuo said. "It's not just 'witch hunts,' but something usually politically driven or used as a way to gain something."

Matsuo said women like Hulda were often marginalized and even persecuted for challenging societal norms. "Given the strong Christian ties in the community at the time, and how religion was certainly weaponized as a means to control the public, something as simple as an unwed woman living alone without kids and trading medicinal herbs with the natives, it could be perceived as a threat to the status quo."

Hieber, coauthor of *A Haunted History of Invisible Women*, said there was "an anxiety, horror, and shame about how out-of-hand the witch trials had gotten in places like Salem" that writers during the 1800s recognized and we are still trying to grapple with even today. "A woman alone has always been suspect throughout history," Hieber said. "Many witch trial victims around the globe were targeted once they became widows."

Hieber said using herbs and folkloric remedies was common across all cultures, "but a woman using this as her sole enterprise, rejecting marriage and children, was often an invitation for societies to vilify her one way or another, regardless of the theological landscape and the exaggerated claims of 'witchcraft' when it was just folk and herbal medicine at work."

Matsuo told me there's another underlying layer to the fictional story of Hulda. "Even though she refused to submit to societal expectations of her time, she submitted her life for the cause. There's a deeper lesson here, almost to the detriment of the community of Sleepy Hollow in that the townspeople were willing to suffer starvation rather than accept food from a kind woman who wasn't Christian or married."

Her martyrdom, Matsuo added, is aligned with the "don't judge a book by its cover" lesson pulled from the pages of a Grimm's fairy tale. "But again, Hulda had to receive fictional 'redemption' not only from the community,

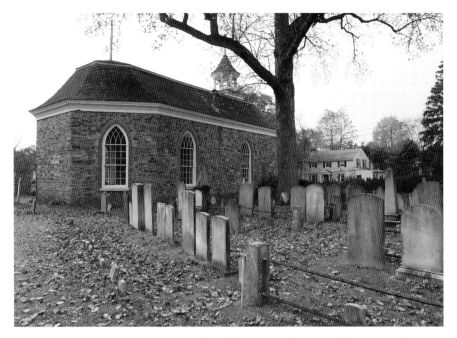

According to Edward Mayhew Bacon's legend, Hulda was laid to rest in an unmarked grave in a remote section of the Old Dutch Church burying ground because she was a witch. *Photo by Angela Artuso.*

but from storytellers by literally dying. Her death was literal, but there are parts of women that 'die' so to speak throughout their lives whether it's a death of their agency or their independence."

Matsuo said the story almost reinforces the idea that a woman has to give up a part of herself in order to be accepted and supported. "In Hulda's case, it was giving up her life," Matsuo said. "For the rest of the women in town, it was either fall in line or be labeled a witch."

As far as Hulda's ghost, it's said her apparition appears near the ruins of her cottage in the woods "with a bag flung over her shoulder and a stick in her hand," according to the October 17, 2017 edition of the *Hudson Independent.*

Of course, the legendary woman's spirit manifests only "on a lonely road during the full moon." While Hulda's fictional backstory has transformed from a minor folk character into a Revolutionary War hero, the ghost lore associated with her has devolved into a witch-on-broom stereotype.

RAVEN ROCK

The most common ghost sighting in Sleepy Hollow? Contrary to popular belief, it's not the Headless Horseman.

According to Jonathan Kruk, the author of *Legends and Lore of Sleepy Hollow and the Hudson Valley*, it's the "wailing woman in white" who haunts the land around Raven Rock.

"In the days of Washington Irving in the early 1800s, it was a forgotten backwater place with swirling eddies which nurtured this xenophobia toward outsiders," Kruk said. "The geography started to stir up ghosts like the wailing woman in white."

Kruk told me that the female spirit is location-bound but explained that she sometimes strays from her postmortem home. He also mentioned that there are several versions to the story behind the ghost that seem to have changed over the years.

"There are three layers to the backstory of the wailing woman in white," he said. "The reason there are so many ghost stories in the region is it is sort of a collective conscious way to recall the Hudson Valley's history. We

Nestled in a far corner of the Rockefeller estate is a massive rock formation known as Raven Rock. *Photo courtesy of demerzel21 from Depositphotos.*

tend to remember past events if there's a ghost involved. With the women in white, the narratives are layered to reflect the different generations."

Kruk said there's one story originating from the Indigenous people of the region that involved a Mohawk warrior trying to capture and sexually assault a Native American woman. "She throws herself off of Raven Rock to escape his clutches. According to the story, the ravens are there to carry off her spirit," Kruk said. "Then there was a woman in colonial times who went to Raven Rock to gather wood and was caught in a blizzard. And before a snowstorm, she's known to ward off people so they don't have a similar fate that she endured."

The most recent iteration of the wailing woman involves a young lady who fell in love with a British soldier during the American Revolution. "The two lovers were planning to meet at Raven Rock. He never came and she ended up freezing to death," Kruk said.

If a ghost is history demanding to be remembered, what do the three different versions mean? "The wailing women in white is a universal ghost story. There's a similar story in all countries and cultures," Kruk told me. "I've looked at this legend in all different ways and I believe the story is buried deep within our subconscious and it somehow manifests as an actual spirit. The underlying theme in all three of these tales seems to be fertility being violated."

As far as the wailing woman in white's home in the woods, Raven Rock is a six-mile hike from the Kykuit mansion and is nestled in the far corner of the Rockefeller estate. The massive stone formation appears to be more of a leaning cliff than an actual rock, but as Kruk explained to me, it's worth the trek to see the hidden gem up close and personal.

"Just looking at the stone at Raven Rock, there's something magical about it," he said, adding that it feels almost like one is transported back in time when they actually hike out to the haunt, which is miles from civilization.

Edgar Mayhew Bacon wrote about the mythical hot spot in his book *Chronicles of Tarrytown and Sleepy Hollow* in 1897. "Raven Rock is a detached portion of the steep, rocky, eastern side of Buttermilk Hill, which a deep fissure has long separated from the mass, and the fragment, becoming independent territory, set up a mythology of its own," Bacon reported.

The story that seems to resonate the most with locals involves the woman who lost her way during a winter storm and froze to death beneath the craggy cliff. "The snow drifted in upon her and she went to sleep never to waken again," Bacon wrote. "Ever since, that cleft has been a melancholy place of refuge, for it is said that the spirit of the poor wayfarer meets the belated wanderer with cries that sound like the screaming of the wind and gestures that remind one of the sweep of snowdrifts, warning others away from the spot that she found so fatal."

For the record, the Raven Rock haunting is one of the ghost stories told at the Van Tassels' party prior to Ichabod Crane's disappearance in "The Legend of Sleepy Hollow." According to Emily Faber in an article published by Sinclair Broadcast Group, "A mention is made of 'the woman in white' that haunted the dark glen at Raven Rock and was often heard to shriek on winter nights before a storm had perished there in the snow."

The backstory of the two additional ghosts in Faber's article published on October 20, 2021, seems to deviate from Kruk's retelling. "It's been suggested that the spot is haunted

Photo of Raven Rock from a collection of photos taken by William A. Owens in *Pocantico Hills, 1609–1959. Photo courtesy of William A. Owens.*

by two additional ghosts, a colonial girl who leaped from the rock to avoid the advances of an unwanted suitor and a Native American woman driven to death by a jealous lover."

It's fairly common for journalists like Faber to mix up the two stories involving the colonial and Native American women. Why? It's likely that the horrible deaths of the ladies were old wives' tales and their stories have been twisted over time.

Leanna Renee Hieber, a New York–based author, told me the color white is significant in ghost lore associated with the female spirits. "In *A Haunted History of Invisible Women*, my co-author Andrea Janes and I touch on this topic as to why these amalgams of women become popular ghost tropes."

Hieber said that the color white is the most common based on her research because "ghosts are often perceived as luminous, pale forms. She may be an innocent or sorrowful figure, appearing in commemoration of an event or tied to specific locations. The women in black are often associated with death, described as widows, a mourning figure or an ill portent."

When Hieber was told that Raven Rock's three women in white are often confused with one another in modern retellings, she wasn't surprised. "No matter the color or aura ascribed to them, their figures evoke a mood in color and movement, but remain entirely devoid of their personhood or identifying details," Hieber said.

Are the ghosts of Raven Rock merely cautionary tales warning the younger generations to stay away from the wilderness or face a similarly tragic fate? Or perhaps the wailing woman in white could be what paranormal researchers call a "harbinger spirit," whose purpose is to warn others of potential danger.

Whether the story is a made-up legend or an actual haunting, the brave souls who venture out to the mysterious Raven Rock insist the land is enchanted, and as the crisp autumn air turns cold, one can hear what sounds like a woman in distress weeping in the woods.

CHAPTER 4

THE HAUNTS

It's a tale of two extremely different, yet oddly similar, Halloween destinations: Salem versus Sleepy Hollow. Will the witches overthrow the Headless Horseman—or will heads roll—in the ultimate Samhain showdown?

According to J.W. Ocker, author of *The New England Grimpendium* and *The New York Grimpendium*, both locations have their "woes" and cons during spooky season.

"I love this topic because depending on how you twist the narrative, you can say these two towns are nothing alike or you can say they are so similar that it's scary," Ocker told me during an in-person interview at the Sleepy Hollow Hotel.

"The number one similarity is that they are both extremely popular Halloween destinations," he said. "You get those clickbait articles every year. Both Salem and Sleepy Hollow are always at the top of every list."

Because they are known for their October attractions, both locations rely heavily on tourism to feed their local economy. "While Salem is changing and becoming more of a suburb of Boston, the bottom line is if they lose their tourism, they will lose their existence."

The author of *A Season with the Witch* added that both cities successfully brand themselves. "No other town can be Salem even though there are tons of other locations that had witch trials, especially in the Northeast. But no one can say they're the Witch City," Ocker said. "Only Salem, Massachusetts, can do that."

Headless Horseman decoration outside of a barbershop in Tarrytown during the Halloween season. *Photo courtesy of James Andrews1 from Shutterstock.*

In comparison, Sleepy Hollow is known for the Headless Horseman. "There are other towns in the country that call themselves Sleepy Hollow, but this area is the only place that can theme themselves around Irving because he actually lived here and was inspired by the region when he wrote the story. It's basically Washington Irving land."

According to Ocker, both Salem and Sleepy Hollow are successful at embracing their respective themes. "There's something about these two Halloween destinations that's authentically spooky," he said. "They're also great fall destinations. The Hudson Valley and New England are top-tier places known for their foliage."

Other similarities include their proximity to major metropolitan areas. "Salem is close to Boston and Sleepy Hollow is a short drive from New York City," he said. "They have this small-town, big-city atmosphere to them. They also have traffic. Who would live in Salem or Sleepy Hollow unless they're spooky, right?"

Another similarity shared by the Witch City and the Hudson Valley seems to be their eerily picturesque cemeteries. "There's the Old Burying Point on Charter Street that almost serves as the hub of Salem in many ways," he told me. "It's even more true in Sleepy Hollow. The cemetery is extremely important. The Old Dutch Church is on the hill, and Washington Irving is buried in the cemetery. The location fits right into Irving's story, and you can almost map out Ichabod Crane's journey."

Speaking of the famous chase from Irving's "The Legend of Sleepy Hollow," Ocker uses the tale as a metaphor to describe the differences between the two tourism-driven destinations. "In my mind, Salem is Ichabod Crane and Sleepy Hollow is the Headless Horseman," he explained. "Salem is so far ahead in regards to marketing themselves, but I feel like the Headless Horseman is slowly creeping up from behind. In most people's minds, Sleepy Hollow is a less evolved version of Salem, but one day it will catch up."

Ocker pointed out that Salem had a huge head start. "The very first Haunted Happenings was in 1982," he explained. "North Tarrytown didn't even become Sleepy Hollow until 1996, so they're almost fifteen years behind Salem."

There's also the obvious geographical hurdles holding back the village. "Sleepy Hollow isn't set up to be a Salem because it simply isn't walkable," he told me. "In Sleepy Hollow, you definitely need a car. In the past, they tried turning the area near the chase statue into a plaza, but the problem is that the street is the same Broadway that's in Manhattan. It's a busy road and it's potentially dangerous to put outside seating or a cafe near the statue. The infrastructure isn't there yet."

For Ocker, Sleepy Hollow's greatest weakness is also what makes it so special. The *OTIS: Odd Things I've Seen* blogger said he prefers celebrating spooky season with his all-time favorite monster, the Headless Horseman. Why? After spending an October in Salem while writing his book *A Season with the Witch*, the New Hampshire–based writer prefers the smaller crowds and the old-school charm of the Hudson Valley.

"In Salem, there's the witch trials tragedy of 1692," he said. "The inciting incident in Sleepy Hollow is just American letters. It's art. So there's no underlying guilt, which is nice. But without that guilt you don't have the friction, the narrative and the interesting public relations angles. The appeal of Salem is a tragedy and in Sleepy Hollow it's just a story."

The lack of an underlying cautionary tale, Ocker told me, also complicates things when it comes to creating paranormal-themed tourism. "Now that Sleepy Hollow is a spooky town, they're trying their best to pull as much haunted content as they can to make it more interesting," he said. "It's really hard to find great ghost stories in Sleepy Hollow, but it was like that in Salem too."

The Witch House was the home of Judge Jonathan Corwin and is one of the few structures standing with direct ties to the Salem witch hysteria of 1692. *Photo courtesy of Paul Brady from Depositphotos.*

Thanks to all of the lantern tours in the Witch City, one can't walk down Essex Street without hitting an allegedly haunted location. In Sleepy Hollow, however, the haunts are definitely spread out.

"There's a passage in 'Legend' where he talks about this Hudson Valley being so haunted," Ocker said. "There are tons of stories and the Headless Horseman is just one example out of all of those tales. In the story, he sets the area up as an interesting place with a lot of legend and lore."

Ocker's recommendations for tourists visiting Sleepy Hollow? "Follow the chase route," he said. "Start at the John André monument and walk to the cemetery. Of course, it's not a very pleasant walk because there are cars whizzing by you. But in October, there's a lot more to do in Sleepy Hollow. It's not every day like it is in Salem, but they have something going on every weekend."

Another telltale sign that Salem is currently in the lead as a Halloween destination? Ocker pointed out that the Witch City's annual Haunted Happenings parade happens at the beginning of October while Sleepy Hollow holds its celebration during the last weekend of the month. "It's very telling who is better at promoting the holiday," he said.

Ocker insisted, however, that New Yorkers are slowly learning to capitalize on the power of the Headless Horseman. "In Sleepy Hollow, you're starting to see recycling bins that are branded. Their fire engines and police cars now have themed logos," he said. "Even the fireplugs are black and orange. If you look around Sleepy Hollow, the Headless Horseman is everywhere."

DARK SHADOWS

When the crew from the American gothic soap opera *Dark Shadows* filmed two movie versions of the supernatural-themed cult classic in the spellbound region in the early 1970s, the monsters of Collinsport gave the Headless Horseman a run for his money.

Vampires, witches and ghosts? Oh my.

Designed in 1838, the stunning Gothic Revival mansion called Lyndhurst served as the exterior set for *House of Dark Shadows* and *Night of Dark Shadows*. Adjacent to Washington Irving's Sunnyside, the country estate was home to former New York City mayor William Paulding, merchant George Merritt and railroad tycoon Jay Gould.

Known as "Paulding's Folly" because the design was asymmetrical and was unfashionable for its time, the mansion is constructed of limestone quarried by prisoners at Sing Sing prison in nearby Ossining, New York.

Lyndhurst's Gothic design elements coupled with its sharply arched windows served as the perfect backdrop for the two *Dark Shadows* flicks. Interior scenes were primarily shot on set at ABC Studios in Manhattan. However, Lyndhurst and several other locations in the area hosted the 175-year-old vampire Barnabas Collins in search of fresh blood and his lost love, Josette.

While there's no denying that Lyndhurst's eerie aesthetic gives it an otherworldly vibe, there oddly aren't many reports of paranormal activity in the turreted mansion overlooking the Hudson River.

"Lyndhurst is not haunted in the traditional sense but there is clearly another dimension to the historic property," wrote Lynda Lee Macken in *Haunted Houses of the Hudson Valley*.

Macken did cite a photographer who has shot thousands of pictures at the Lyndhurst estate over the years and picked up "bursts of blue light" in several of his photographs. The paranormal-themed writer mentioned that these light anomalies could be "the essence of spirits manifesting in our mortal world."

Lyndhurst, also known as the Jay Gould estate, is a Gothic Revival country house that sits in its own sixty-seven-acre park beside the Hudson River. *Photo by Sam Baltrusis.*

The author also noted that "one of the resulting photos shows a lake with a castle positioned in the background. Subsequent research revealed that decades ago a pond did indeed exist at the spot."

There's another story involving a "little ghost girl" haunting the land behind Lyndhurst near the Hudson River. "Dressed in a white frock, visitors mentioned hearing a small child's laugh and seeing a ghost girl hiding behind trees and bushes," wrote Macken. "When her appearance is investigated nobody is there. Some say she is the child of one of the former owners," adding that "it's alleged the girl drowned in the Hudson River."

In an interesting side note, the Old Croton Aqueduct Trail passes through the Lyndhurst estate and crosses next to Washington Irving's Sunnyside. For those looking to explore the region on foot, the path also connects to other haunted locations in the region, including the Armour-Stiner Octagon House in Irvington.

In addition to Lyndhurst, the crew from *Dark Shadows* filmed in Sleepy Hollow Cemetery, where one of the mausoleum-style receiving vaults was transformed into the long-term resting place for the movie's blood-sucking lead played by Jonathan Frid.

On a recent tour in the Sleepy Hollow Cemetery, the guide Cristina Lombardi was able to open up the crypt used by the crew from the *Dark Shadows* movies. The space occupied by Frid's vampire character featured a movie still of Barnabas Collins next to a plastic skull. In the film, Barnabas

A crypt in Sleepy Hollow Cemetery served as the home of vampire Barnabas Collins during the filming of two *Dark Shadows* movies. *Photo by Sam Baltrusis.*

was entombed in a secret room at the rear of the mausoleum. It was only accessible by pulling the ring in the lion's mouth over the center grave plaque.

When asked if she's heard of any paranormal activity near the crypt in the Sleepy Hollow Cemetery, Lombardi quickly said "no." The structure was only used as a receiving vault, or a holding area designed to temporarily store skeletal remains in the winter months when the ground is frozen. The tour guide told me the bodies spend only a short time in the tomb before they are buried in the cemetery.

In the movie, the town troublemaker Willie Loomis drives down to the Collins family mausoleum hoping to find buried treasures in the tomb. He locates a hidden switch that opens a secret antechamber. In the crypt, there is a large stone coffin wrapped in heavy iron chains, and he manages to pry them open. Instead of treasure, Loomis finds the Collins family vampire, who quickly grabs the young man by the neck and drinks his blood.

Under Barnabas's spell, Loomis refurbishes the original Collins family home called the Old House. An abandoned mansion in Tarrytown known as the Spratt House served as the fanged patriarch's home in the movies. It was convenient for the film crew because the mansion built by Moses Hicks Grinnell in the 1850s was a stone's throw to Lyndhurst.

Soon after filming *House of Dark Shadows*, the old mansion caught on fire, and only the charred remnants of its foundation remained.

As far as additional paranormal reports from the waterfront property used for the *Dark Shadows* movies, there is a tale of "an intoxicated villager" who lost his balance and drowned while attempting to navigate his makeshift vessel across the Tappan Zee section of the Hudson River. According to Jerry Eimbinder in the September 30, 2011 edition of the *Tarrytown–Sleepy Hollow Patch*, "Boaters say he often waves to passing vessels."

Meanwhile, the team at Lyndhurst has embraced its *Dark Shadows* past. They've hosted several events over the years celebrating its ties to the Collins clan, including meet and greets with some of the actors who appeared on both the TV series and the two movies filmed at the mansion. During the Halloween season, they offer a nighttime tour called "Lyndhurst After Dark" where they take a painting of Barnabas Collins out of storage and put it on display and showcase other items associated with the mansion's darker history.

No word if the spirits from Lyndhurst's past come out to play—like the ghost girl who allegedly haunts the shoreline behind the mansion—when the veil between the living and dead has lifted.

HOLY GHOSTS

Out of all of the real locations mentioned in Washington Irving's "The Legend of Sleepy Hollow," the Old Dutch Church and its historic graveyard are arguably the short story's most iconic. In fact, thousands of visitors flock to the spot where the Headless Horseman supposedly tethered his sinister steed nightly among the graves in its churchyard.

Aerial view of the Old Dutch Church in Sleepy Hollow, New York, during the winter. *Photo courtesy of by Fhougue from iStock.*

But is it haunted?

"The ghostly activity associated with the Old Dutch Church is concentrated mainly on the cemetery on its grounds. The cemetery is as old as the church itself, making it one of the oldest cemeteries in the United States," reported Erin Egnatz in the *Haunting Around America* blog. "The most famous ghost in the cemetery is that of the Headless Horseman. Just as in Irving's story, though his story was fiction, it was said to be based on the ghost that roams the old burial grounds. The headless specter is said to be a military officer who fought in the Revolution when his head was shot clear off due to cannon fire. According to some, he still prowls the church in hopes of finding his lost head."

The online post from September 3, 2020, continued, "Others say he is still on patrol, completely ignoring the fact he is minus a head. It appears as though the ghost never leaves the grounds, remaining confined to the land of the cemetery."

However, naysayers like author Alex Matsuo told me that the ghost stories associated with the Old Dutch Church's burial ground and the adjoining Sleepy Hollow Cemetery are likely a bunch of horsefeathers.

"Personally, I don't believe that cemeteries are constantly haunted by the people who are buried there," Matsuo said. "But just as living people visit cemeteries, I would venture to guess that the dead also visit cemeteries. Perhaps they want to pay their respects to a comrade or even a celebrity that they never had a chance to meet in life."

If the grave has been desecrated or is unmarked, she said, it's possible that the spirit is sticking around because of unfinished business.

Paranormal investigators like Angela Artuso told me that there's a local legend that the headless Hessian who was killed in battle was interred in a clearing in between the Old Dutch Church's burial ground and Sleepy Hollow Cemetery. If the skeletal remains of a decapitated Hessian soldier are somewhere on the property, it could explain why his spirit was spotted roaming among the graves.

"He's said to be buried in an area where there are no headstones and is unmarked," Artuso said, adding that it's possible that the soldier entombed in the makeshift grave could have inspired Irving for his main antagonist. "With all of this energy swirling around the burial ground and Sleepy Hollow Cemetery, it doesn't surprise me at all that one would hear voices from those who have passed on and even an apparition or two."

Construction began on the Old Dutch Church and the burial ground in the 1680s. During the American Revolution, the land was seized by New York because the family who owned it remained loyal to the British. The church was renovated at the end of the 1700s and was nearly destroyed in a fire in the 1830s, but the structure has persevered and continues to hold Sunday services during the summer months.

There are several reports of a female spirit haunting the cemetery as well. Todd Atteberry, author of *Haunted Travels in the Hudson River Valley of Washington Irving*, spotted an apparition while taking photos of the Old Dutch Church. "I got the shot and as I lowered the camera from my eye, for a fraction of a second, there was someone standing a few feet to my right, in full colonial-era garb," he wrote. "My mind flashed to the thought that it was a re-enactor from Philipsburg Manor across the road, which

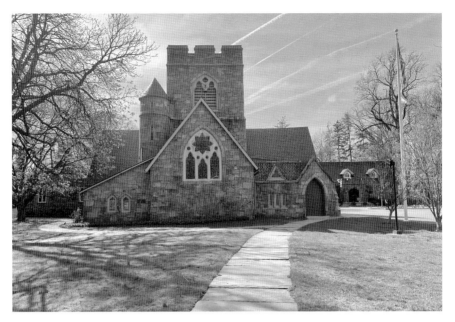

The Church of St. Barnabas is an Episcopal house of worship in Irvington, New York. *Photo by Sam Baltrusis.*

allowed me to catch my breath at least, except in that same instant, I also saw that I was alone."

While the Old Dutch Church is the spellbound region's most recognizable place of worship, it's not the Hudson Valley's most haunted.

Over at the Church of St. Barnabas in Irvington, the Episcopal rectory dates back to the 1850s. It's believed to be "haunted by the spirit of its founder, John McVickar, as well as a woman who may have been his wife," reported the *New York Haunted Houses* website. "The female ghost is drawn to the children of pastors who live in the rectory and will often visit them at night."

The truth behind the paranormal activity has been twisted a bit online. The male spirit isn't the founder of St. Barnabas, while the identity of the female specter is up for debate.

The church was originally supposed to serve as a school, and McVickar purchased the land to be close to his good friend and benefactor Irving. The plan was to build a school and chapel, but the idea was eventually scrapped, and it was then established as a parish for the Episcopal Church.

McVickar's son, William, was appointed as the first pastor of St. Barnabas. It was his apparition that chased out a crew of workers installing a new organ in 2000. Parishioners believe it was William, and not his father, John, spotted in the church's sanctuary.

As far as the female spirit, most of the reported incidents took place during the thirty-six-year stint when the Reverend Charles Colwell lived in the rectory with his wife, Judy, and their three daughters.

Their youngest child, Amanda, was looking through old photographs from the church's archives with her mother one day and noticed an old sepia-toned picture of a woman in a Victorian-era dress.

"That's her!" Amanda said according to the October 2, 2011 edition of the *Hudson Independent*. "That's the woman who sits in the chair in my room at night. But she never says anything."

According to the article by Barrett Seaman, "The woman in the picture was Mrs. Isabel Benjamin, who lived in the rectory from 1867 to 1907—a century before Amanda was born. There was apparently nothing Amanda found menacing in her presence—just a reluctance to speak while she sat in the corner of her bedroom, knitting."

The resident spirit was married to McVickar's successor, also named William, who presided over the rectory for forty years.

There have been no ghostly sightings reported since 2000, but one parishioner named Barbara Wright told the *Hudson Independent* that "she distinctly felt some unseen presence brush past her as she ascended the parish hall staircase one day," the report noted. "Yet it cannot be said with certainty whether the spirits have vacated the premises or just slipped back into obscurity."

Even if the paranormal activity returns to St. Barnabas, churchgoers shouldn't be alarmed.

Richard Estep, a veteran investigator and a prolific author, told me he hasn't experienced a negative or aggressive haunting at a place of worship after almost thirty years of research in the field. "Churches are by their nature spiritual places, where quiet contemplation of the greater questions of existence takes place," he told me. "Many church hauntings involve people who loved those places very much during their lifetimes and tend to linger behind for a while, or somehow leave a small part of themselves behind whenever they move on."

PATRIOT'S PARK

The ghosts of the American Revolution continue to haunt the Hudson River Valley. One of the region's more notorious legends from the era involves the capture and execution of Major John André, a British intelligence officer apprehended on September 23, 1780, in an outdoor space near the Tarrytown and Sleepy Hollow line known as Patriot's Park.

Tales of André's spirit lingering near an "enormous tulip-tree" creep out the fictional Ichabod Crane in Washington Irving's classic story. The brief mention in "The Legend of Sleepy Hollow," however, was based on actual reports of a residual playback of the action that had occurred forty years before Irving penned his tale.

After an evening of storytelling at the Van Tassels', Crane passes by what was known as Major André's tree, which towers "like a giant above all the other trees of the neighborhood," Irving penned. Its larger-than-life presence and tragic association with the British spy's execution had earned it "a mixture of respect and superstition, partly out of sympathy for the fate of its ill-starred namesake, and partly from the tales of strange sights, and doleful lamentations, told concerning it."

As Crane gallops past the tree toward the Headless Horseman's bridge, "he heard a groan—his teeth chattered, and his knees smote against the saddle." Was it, as Irving wrote in "The Legend of Sleepy Hollow," merely "the rubbing of one huge bough upon another other," or was it actually André's ghost?

The major was engaged in secret negotiations with Benedict Arnold for the surrender of West Point. Returning to New York after the liaison, André was captured by three Patriots after he mistook one of them as a Hessian. The British officer was then ferried across the Hudson to Tappan and tried for espionage, convicted and tragically hanged on October 2, 1780.

Edgar Mayhew Bacon in *Chronicles of Tarrytown and Sleepy Hollow* wrote about a residual haunting near where the major was captured. "Down the post road, on still autumn nights, belated wayfarers sometimes heard the sound of hoofs. A madly galloping horse seemed to approach, but no horse or horseman was visible to the keenest eyes," Bacon wrote. "All agreed that the hoofbeats stopped as though the rider had reined in suddenly, and that they were never heard further south than the immense old tulip tree, known as André's tree, that spread its gaunt ghost-like arms in the moonlight."

Like many of the characters in "The Legend of Sleepy Hollow," there was some truth behind the lore associated with André's tree.

Patriot's Park features a statue commemorating the capture by John Paulding and his fellow Patriots Isaac Van Wart and David Williams of the British spy John André. *Photo by Sam Baltrusis.*

According to Katherine Egner Gruber's blog post on the Jamestown-Yorktown Foundation's website, "There really was a tree rumored to have an association with André, most notably cataloged by Irving's friend and sometimes collaborator James Kirke Paulding in his 1828 New York travelogue, *The New Mirror for Travellers.*"

Patriot's Park is located on U.S. Route 9 along the boundary between Tarrytown and Sleepy Hollow in Westchester County, New York. *Photo courtesy of Paul Brady from Depositphotos.*

Paulding wrote about the memory of a large tulip tree, "one hundred and eleven feet and a half high, the limbs projecting on either side more than eighty feet from the trunk, which was ten paces round." According to Paulding, local tradition held that it was under this very tree where Patriots first apprehended and searched Major John André before delivering him across the Hudson River to meet his fate.

The tree was reportedly destroyed by lightning about twenty years after the British major's execution and ten years before Irving wrote his famous short story. Adding even more fuel to the mystery, André's tree was struck around the time Benedict Arnold died in June 1801.

The residual haunting continued for more than a century, and apparently André's ghost has a calendar. "Eyewitnesses never report seeing anything here, but the sounds of his ride were reported year after year on the anniversary of the famous capture," wrote Emma G. on the *Sleepy Hollow Country* blog. "Not content to wail and moan near the site of the gallows, it would seem that John André's ghost instead returns to Tarrytown, again and again, to try and succeed in his mission. Each time, he fails and is doomed to repeat it again."

The blogger mentioned that "as with many ghosts, as the years go by the recollections fade and the sightings dwindle to nothing."

In other words, the residual haunting associated with André's ghost had an expiration date.

Brian J. Cano from *Paranormal Caught on Camera* and *The Haunted Collector* told me that psychic imprints can be exacerbated by the living. "We're constantly expending energy and leaving bits of ourselves behind," he said. "These sorts of things are the basic building blocks of an echo."

Certain locations, however, will continue to "reenergize" their residual hauntings thanks to period actors and a continued remembrance of the events that shaped our nation.

"Reenactors are very dedicated to their performances," he explained. "When they're in uniform, they are out for blood and that energy can be left behind. The battle is replayed over and over again, and I believe the spirits are re-energized because of it."

Cano said he wasn't surprised that a playback haunting like the capture of Major André diminished over time. "The ghosts from the Revolutionary War will dissipate and we'll start talking to ghosts from the twentieth century," he told me. "As we move forward in our timeline, the energy also moves forward."

As a seasoned investigator, Cano said it's important to use caution when attempting to communicate with ghosts from André's era. "The minute you start investigating, you're sending a signal to the astral plane that you're attempting to make contact with the spirit realm," he said. "When we send out that signal, you never know who or what is responding."

If investigators claim that they're communicating with the more well-known ghosts associated with the American Revolution like André or Arnold, Cano told me that it may be wishful thinking. "If someone is trying to contact George Washington and they get a response, they're going to automatically think it's him," he said. "How would they know what George Washington sounded like? There's no logic behind that approach. People try to connect the dots too quickly."

Tourists often visit Patriot's Park, where American militiamen arrested André and found incriminating papers stuffed into his boots. The mysterious tree that marked the spot is long gone. But why have the phantom noises of André's capture faded over time?

"Perhaps it is the busy cars on what was the old road drowning out the sound of hoofbeats, or perhaps the more we forget, the more the spook begins to fade; as if the haunting is only as present as memory is," reported Emma G. for the *Sleepy Hollow Country* website. "Or, because this is Sleepy Hollow, there is only room for one phantom horseman galloping the streets searching in vain for something that is lost."

SCHOOL SPIRITS

When it comes to haunted schools, Sleepy Hollow and Tarrytown have more than their fair share of them. Spine-chilling tales of unexplained sounds, flickering lights, residual apparitions and levitating objects have become a rite of passage for the uninitiated high school or college freshman adapting to life in one of the haunted classrooms scattered throughout the Hudson River Valley.

Elizabeth Tucker, a professor of English at Binghamton University and author of *Haunted Halls: Ghostlore of American College Campuses*, said that campus ghost stories are morality plays for the modern era. "They educate freshmen about how to live well in college," she explained in a 2007 interview, adding that the cautionary tales serve as spooky metaphors of fear, disorder and insanity. They also reflect students' interest in their school's historical legacy. Yep, campus ghost lore is a paranormal pep rally of sorts. "You don't find ghost stories at schools without a sense of pride," Tucker continued. "School spirits reflect school spirit."

Richard Estep, author of *A Haunting at Farrar* and a veteran paranormal investigator, believes the coming-of-age stress that's unleashed in high school and college campuses can leave a psychic imprint.

"For some, school days are the best days of their lives. For others, they are a living hell from which they cannot wait to escape," Estep told me. "In each instance, there is a strong emotion, be it positive or negative. Where one finds intense emotion, one also tends to find ghosts. I believe that's why we see so many cases of haunted schools."

The students at Sleepy Hollow High, for example, were convinced that the light at the top of one of the building's towers was controlled by a ghost, noting that the light changes often and randomly. "Do they know about the friendly ghost of Margaret Howard next door at 200 N. Broadway? School employees have reported seeing her over the years in the upper story of the building," reported Maria Ann Roglieri in the October 3, 2017 edition of the *Hudson Independent*. "Do the students know about the ghost of a sad young woman who reportedly haunts the attic of the same building, having thrown herself out the window to her death when she was working in the dress factory?"

The school district's administration building, located next to Sleepy Hollow High, was built in 1909 and was known for years as the Edward Harden Mansion. It's reportedly haunted by Margaret Howard, a wealthy dressmaker who owned the building more than a century ago. She's been

Historic postcard of Tarrytown High School and Second Reformed Church printed by the Albertype Company. *Courtesy of Card Cow.*

spotted walking the upper floors, while the young woman who supposedly plunged to her death haunts the attic.

Howard never actually lived in the mansion. She was an Irish immigrant who became a successful dressmaker in Manhattan. She passed away in 1926 and bequeathed her millions to purchase and maintain a home for retired seamstresses like those who had worked for her in the city. The property was managed by the Sisters of Mercy, and many of the women living there sewed uniforms for American troops during World War II. The Edward Harden Mansion was sold to Tarrytown's school district in 1955 and then briefly served as a private school for boys.

While the story of the distressed female spirit lingering in the building's attic hasn't been validated, it's important to point out that Sleepy Hollow High has embraced its haunted heritage. Their official mascot, for instance, is the Horseman. The school has adopted Irving's headless Hessian as its own and proudly showcases the galloping ghoul at pep rallies and football games.

They got spirits, yes they do.

Students at EF International Academy in Tarrytown may be studying under the ghostly gaze of Mother Butler and Father Gailhac, who co-founded the campus's previous institution of Marymount. There are also reports of a haunted parking lot on campus where an old dormitory once stood.

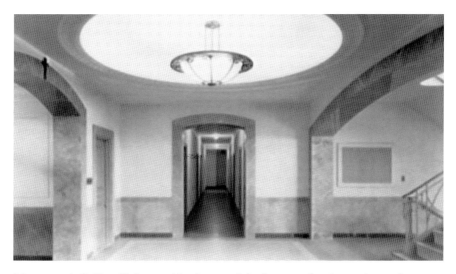

Marymount's Gailhac Hall was said to be one of the former college's most haunted dormitories. *Photo courtesy of the Library of Congress.*

Marymount has been closed since 2007, but the *Haunted Places* blog reported that Gailhac and Butler "roam the halls of the dorms and protect the girls of this women's college," the post explained. "Evil spirits lurk in Sacky parking lot. Strange phenomena exist in these halls from invisible bed guests to bed shaking and the constant feeling of being watched."

An employee who worked at the EF International Academy agreed that the campus was haunted and commented that they "saw a shadowy figure move from right to left. It was awesome and I also heard whistling."

Another anonymous source mentioned that Father Gailhac passed before the college was built. Butler, on the other hand, was buried in a crypt on the Marymount campus. "In my years at Marymount, I can't say I ever met her wandering around, but I know she was very much loved by students who knew her when she was alive," the anonymous source commented.

The former student also added that the "Sacky" dormitory was actually called Sacre Coeur Hall. "It was one of our favorite dorms because it was a nice old mansion with turrets and a wide veranda with a view of the Hudson River. Haunted? I doubt it. In any case, if there are 'spirits' slouching around the parking lot, they're benevolent ones."

Other graduates insisted that the campus lived up to its paranormally active reputation. One alum lived in room 404 at Gailhac Hall from 1982 to 1986 and "witnessed apparitions of a female in a white, poet-like dress walking down the hall only to disappear into the wall. This happened on two occasions and never again."

A student named Virginia who studied English at EF International Academy during the summer of 2009 claimed she heard a terrifying guttural voice say, "Give me your soul," and then was startled by the disembodied cries of a woman as she ran down the stairs. "This has been one of the worst paranormal experiences I have ever had," she added.

Why would Sleepy Hollow High and former dorms at Marymount College be haunted? Joni Mayhan, author of *When Ghosts Are Near*, told me that negative energies are often attracted to the extreme emotions emanating from students.

"In the case of a high school, I think it also has a lot to do with the type of energy it is filled with. Teenagers have spiky hormonal energy that ghosts like to feed on," she told me. "It's no coincidence that most poltergeist cases are a result of teens living in a haunted building. Imagine having an entire building filled with teenagers and you've created a ghost buffet."

CHAPTER 5

THE NIGHTLIFE

The spellbound region boasts a motley crew of nightlife locales rumored to be stomping grounds for the spirits—and not the kind served on the rocks. The list includes a bevy of atypical haunts, ranging from an upscale restaurant located inside one of New York's most haunted mansions to the historic Tarrytown Music Hall on Main Street.

Apparently, the living aren't the only things that go bump in the nightlife.

Historically, the watering holes in the Hudson Valley were gathering places for American Revolution–era Patriots and were, in essence, "nerve centers for spreading vital news and sanctuaries for outlawed organizations," wrote Roxie Zwicker in *Haunted Pubs of New England*. "Certain pubs bore witness to ghastly deeds and sorrowful tragedies," Zwicker continued. "Some of them became tinged with the aura of the supernatural."

Angela Artuso, a Long Island–based author and founder of Gotham Paranormal, told me that there's an "aura of disaster" lingering in the area. "There's definitely a psychic imprint on the land," she said. "Sleepy Hollow itself holds such a large amount of history, especially during the Revolutionary War period and all of that energy has carried over through the years."

Stuck right in the middle of the colonies, the Hudson River Valley served as a nexus for the conflict and hosted many key figures, battles and political events over an eight-year period.

Artuso said the extreme emotions from more than two centuries ago set the stage for potential paranormal activity.

Historic photo of Tarrytown's Main Street taken between 1910 and 1920. *Photo courtesy of the Detroit Publishing Company.*

"The inns and taverns in Sleepy Hollow were at one time used as command stations, prisoner holding areas and meeting places during the Revolutionary War period," she said. "The entire land was occupied at that time."

And then there's the aftermath of the war, which indirectly gave birth to America's first monster. The popularity of "The Legend of Sleepy Hollow" continues to serve as a major catalyst that seems to amplify ghostly sightings reported in the region.

Artuso suggested that Washington Irving brought the Headless Horseman to life when he wrote the tale in 1820. "If you consider how many years and generations that the story has been told, it has become almost a part of history," she said. "If you think of something so often, at some point it can become real. Could it be only in one's mind and be transformed into pareidolia? Yes, absolutely."

In other words, paranormal enthusiasts looking for an encounter with the Headless Horseman will likely find him whether it's an actual haunting or not.

When asked if other entities could assume the role of Irving's famous phantom, she told me that it's very unlikely based on her experience in the field. "I don't think there would be any entity in particular that would want to mimic the Headless Horseman," she said.

Artuso also mentioned the possibility of a thought-form manifestation conjured by the thousands of tourists who flock to Sleepy Hollow each year. "You have all of these people saying they've seen the Headless Horseman galloping through the cemetery; it could be that the collective vision of that scenario actually 'created' the sighting and brought life to it," she explained. "It's very much like the Philip Experiment that was conducted in the early 1970s."

For the record, parapsychologists in Toronto, Canada, set up a study to determine whether subjects can communicate with a fictionalized ghost that was in essence created. Their goal was to make up a character using a science-based methodology, and then the group attempted to communicate with it through a séance. The experiment apparently worked, and participants were convinced they experienced paranormal activity associated with the fictional character named "Philip Aylesford."

While the experiment proved that thought-forms can actually be a viable possibility, contemporary reports of decapitated spirits have mysteriously popped up outside of Sleepy Hollow and Tarrytown.

Tarrytown Music Hall is located on West Main Street in the downtown area. *Photo courtesy of appalachianview from Depositphotos.*

Ken Summers reported in the October 13, 2014 edition of *Week in Weird* that "a headless Hessian in full uniform" was spotted on Mount Airy Road near Teller's Point. The author also mentioned a firsthand encounter on Albany Post Road at the Rogers-Haight Homestead. According to the story, the ghostly figure lost his head in an argument with another soldier over a pig.

Has Artuso seen the Headless Horseman? Nope. However, she did have a few inexplicable experiences over the years. In fact, her team has investigated several of Sleepy Hollow's nightlife haunts, including the Tarrytown Music Hall. She even felt like she was being watched by something unseen while having lunch at J.P. Doyle's on Beekman Avenue.

"You can definitely feel a presence when you enter," she said about the popular restaurant known for its "Horseman" burger. "It was very strange, and you could feel something present near the bar area heading into the restroom."

Artuso told me that there's an emotional energy embedded within many of Sleepy Hollow's haunted hot spots. "If you think about all of the happiness, sadness, fear and excitement at these locations," she said, "all of that energy ends up getting absorbed into the environment which can potentially result in a haunting."

GOOSEFEATHER

The ghost of Sybil Harris King is said to haunt the Tarrytown House Estate's King Mansion, home to the Cantonese-style eatery called Goosefeather.

Raven Rock's wailing spirit? Watch your back. There's a new white-dressed woman in town.

Sybil was the wife of Frederick King, whose father was vice president of the Baltimore & Ohio Railroad and owner of what was originally called Uplands when it was built in 1840, now known as King Mansion.

The lady of the house died in 1955 on the second floor of the Georgian-style home. King's deathbed is one flight up from Goosefeather restaurant, co-founded by Dale Talde from *Top Chef*.

"She has been heard pacing up and down the second-floor hallways and tends to linger near Room 293, the room she is said to have passed away in," reported the *Haunted History Trail of New York State*'s website. "Sometimes Sybil will even appear as an apparition in white, or show herself through sounds, orbs, and faint shadows to guests staying in her former home."

Goosefeather is located in the first floor of the Tarrytown House Estate's King Mansion. *Photo by Angela Artuso.*

One of the bartenders at Goosefeather told me that Sybil often makes her way down to the first floor and interacts with patrons in the restaurant. In fact, the employee, who wishes to remain anonymous, said she had a face-to-face experience with a ghostly presence in the kitchen area. "I'm not sure if it was Sybil and I'm not even sure if it was male or female, but it was definitely something," she said, adding that she swore someone—or something—passed by the kitchen doors, but no one was there.

The bartender told me that the resident ghost often plays with the staff, adding that "glasses and silverware often get thrown from the bar."

Angela Artuso, the founder of Gotham Paranormal, told me that she hasn't had a personal encounter with Sybil when she visited the restaurant in the past, but she has heard several convincing stories from employees who have.

"Apparently, there was a couple that visited and ate at Goosefeather at the end of their stay at the Tarrytown House Estate," Artuso told me. "They had such a great time and such a wonderful meal that when the check came, they decided to keep the hardcover book that came with their bill thinking no one would really mind since they had so many."

Goosefeather's main dining room area looks like a library at a historic manor, with aged books scattered on the shelves coupled with several fireplaces. After dining, the waitstaff often slips the check into one of the books taken from the King Mansion library.

According to Artuso, one couple made the mistake of taking the hardcover home with them.

"On their way out, their GPS kept rerouting their trip back to the restaurant," she said. "No matter how many times they tried to clear it, they kept getting rerouted. The couple started to get the feeling that someone or something at the restaurant wanted the book back, so they headed back to Goosefeather and returned the book. Once it was returned, their GPS took them home without any further rerouting."

Books from the King Mansion's library are used to deliver Goosefeather's bills. *Photo by Angela Artuso.*

Joni Mayhan, author of *Dark and Scary Things*, told me that it's fairly common for spirits to protect what was once their property, especially if the book was taken from the library of the mansion's previous owner.

"We know from past experiences that ghosts often attach to more than the homes they lived in," Mayhan explained. "Sometimes they attach themselves to their favorite items. I've found that tools, toys, clothing, furniture and even weapons are prime candidates for a haunting. Books could easily fit into this category as well."

Mayhan said that it could also simply be indignation from one of the protector spirits at the mansion. "Imagine haunting your favorite location and watching someone steal something and walk away with it," Mayhan said. "People usually don't realize that ghosts can be that 'fly on the wall.' They hang around, completely invisible and watch the comings and goings of the establishment. If they watch someone steal something, they might feel compelled to react."

The author and paranormal investigator joked that the scenario at King Mansion makes her want to be a ghost in the future. "After I get finished at my ex-husband's house, I might be compelled to haunt my favorite establishment too," she said with a laugh.

As far as the apparition's all-white outfit, Mayhan said women from Sybil's generation often wore floor-length dresses. "If you saw a female ghost from that era, her most defining feature would probably be her dress. It is interesting to me that so many of the historical female ghosts we see are dressed in white," she said. "In their day, white was a color they probably wouldn't have worn frequently due to the difficulty of keeping it clean. They didn't have dry cleaning services back then. A dress would have been worn many times before it was cleaned, which meant a white dress would have looked dirtier faster than a darker-colored fabric. Either the dress was a wedding dress or bed clothing, or the color of the dress is symbolic. White often is associated with purity."

The bartender at Goosefeather said the spirit haunting the King Mansion seems to be benevolent in nature. However, she believes there's another ghost haunting the Biddle Mansion located on the other side of the property. It's a picturesque stone structure where breakfast is served to guests staying at the Tarrytown House Estate.

"The spirit at the King Mansion is playful, but the energy over at the Mary Duke Ballroom is very stern and kind of judgmental," she said, adding that she believes the spirit haunting the Biddle Mansion is its previous owner.

The Tarrytown House Estate includes two mansions formerly owned by Mary Duke Biddle, the daughter of Benjamin Duke, who co-founded Duke University and the Duke Tobacco Company. The heiress purchased the stone mansion in 1921 and then purchased the King estate in 1959 following Sybil's passing.

Mayhan told me that if Biddle was a hard-to-please person when she was alive, the trait could have continued in the afterlife. "I believe that the personalities people have during life follow them into death," she said. "If someone was a negative person, they would probably become a fairly miserable ghost. Compounding this is the fact that Mary was a former homeowner. If she was fastidious in tending to the house, she might be resentful over seeing someone else doing what she can no longer do."

OLD '76 HOUSE

Want to dine with the spirits? Take a trip across the Hudson River to the Old '76 House in Tappan, New York, where British spy Major John André—who conspired with the notorious traitor Benedict Arnold—was jailed before his execution by hanging on October 2, 1780.

Built in 1668, the Old '76 House served as the spellbound region's nerve center during the American Revolution and even hosted the country's first president, George Washington, when he was commander-in-chief of the Continental army.

Nicknamed "André's Prison" and originally called Mabie's Inn, the tavern was turned into a makeshift jail for André, who was captured near modern-day Patriot's Park. He was then ferried over the Tappan Zee and was put on trial for espionage at the Reformed Church next to the Old '76 House, where he was imprisoned, and then hanged on a hill behind the tavern.

According to Robert Norden, who restored the restaurant to its original glory when his family purchased the property in 1987, the ghostly activity at the Old '76 House is hard to ignore. "We'll all be doing a staff meeting in the other room and you'll hear a glass fall off the table," he told Kevin Phelan from the *Journal News* on May 14, 2016. "Nobody even bothers getting up anymore because it's always that a glass fell off of table two and they never break. So you just pick it up, put it back."

Norden said he was skeptical of the paranormal activity at first, but his opinion changed after decades of hard-to-explain encounters. "He's seen a preponderance of evidence—from staff, customers and paranormal experts alike—that the hamlet eatery might be housing some guests of the ghostly variety, despite whatever healthy skepticism he harbors," the journalist wrote.

One of the resident spirits reportedly hovers around one of the tables in the tavern and counts silver coins. Employees often find misplaced dimes near the haunted area. In fact, one waitress was shocked when a dime fell from the ceiling and landed on her book when she was sitting at table two at the Old '76 House.

In the area where André was held prisoner, Norden noticed a man dressed in a white shirt sitting back in the table's chairs. "A bartender saw him, too, and, assuming he was staying for an after-dinner drink, began reaching for a bottle," reported the *Journal News*.

A member of the waitstaff heard what sounded like a disembodied sigh behind her back while she was setting up the bar. When she turned around to look for the source of the noise, she was shocked to learn that her boss wasn't in the room. "She came to Norden with her experience, at which point he informed her that that day was the anniversary of André's hanging," Phelan noted in the article.

Angela Artuso from Gotham Paranormal told me that the residual energy seems to intensify around the anniversary of André's execution.

The Old '76 House is a colonial-era structure originally built as a home and tavern in Tappan, New York. *Photo by Angela Artuso.*

According to legend, a picture of Benedict Arnold was turned upside down by an upset George Washington at the Old '76 House. *Photo by Angela Artuso.*

The investigator and sensitive also added that she strongly believes that the British spy left a psychic imprint at the tavern.

"He left a lasting impression to the point where I really felt like I felt his presence around us," she told me after having lunch at the restaurant. "And to see the room where he was held felt so heavy. Even touching the door that led to that room resonated a very heavy vibe. Everything in the Old '76 House gave off a tremendous amount of energy including the fireplace we sat next to with the original portrait of Benedict Arnold that was deliberately placed upside down by George Washington."

Joni Mayhan, author of *Dark and Scary Places*, believes the historic nature of the Old '76 House adds fuel to the ghostly fire. "In recent years, I've become fascinated with liminal spaces. They are places where people move through in masses," Mayhan told me. "Take for example a haunted highway or a haunted inn. Many people pass through there over the years, creating something similar to a vortex of energy. We see many haunted hospitals, taverns and public buildings. Another example is a staircase. We often see residual ghosts appear walking up them as they did in life."

Both Artuso and Mayhan take more of an empathic approach to the paranormal, while Ron Yacovetti, a trailblazer in the field who crafted a white noise spirit communication device he calls Staticom, has a more scientific explanation for the activity happening at the Old '76 House.

"The last time I investigated the Old '76 House was around 2015, and we did seem to get a regular stream of responses from a spirit box at a table within the main dining area that is said to be haunted," Yacovetti told me. "Also EMF sensors had shown several 'on command' reactions around that same area and table."

While Yacovetti agreed that the activity at the tavern was more residual in nature, he's not sold on the idea that there's a psychological imprint at the Old '76 House.

"John André surely suffered in that environment and that would impact his psyche and overall mental state during his life. The idea of an emotion being imprinted onto a physical environment is not what makes most sense if scientifically examined," he told me. "But continuity of consciousness influencing the transpersonal state of an environment associated with the trauma most certainly does."

The Old '76 House served as a makeshift prison for British spy John André before he was executed by hanging. *Photo by Angela Artuso.*

Yacovetti investigated with a group called Ghost Hunts USA back in 2015 that has since disbanded. The event organizer, Josh Taylor, told the *Daily Voice* newspaper on October 3, 2016, that people reported seeing a man dressed in military-style clothing, like a redcoat uniform, and full-bodied apparitions in the area used as André's prison.

"People in the room have seen apparitions walking through the walls and when they walked over to look for themselves there would be nobody there," Taylor told Donna Christopher at the *Daily Voice*. "People could sit in there and it could be very warm, yet they go stone cold in the room."

In addition to Taylor, the journalist interviewed the former general manager of the Old '76 House Rudy Zayas. The longtime employee had several experiences working at the tavern, including one spine-tingling story after last call. "I was turning the lights off and it was just me and the bartender still here. After I turned off the light I saw a man sitting at a table in the front of the dining room," Zayas recalled. "I told her to buy him a drink and turned the light back on for the customer. She turned to me and said, 'There's no one there.'"

Was it André's ghost? Artuso is convinced that the ghost of the American Revolution–era spy is still lingering at the tavern where he was held prisoner. "I believe his spirit is there," she told me. "I feel as though he wants us to know his story."

SPIRITED PUBS

There are two taverns in Tarrytown—J.P. Doyle's and Set Back Inn—that are said to be haunted by thirsty patrons who will materialize out of thin air and sometimes even motion for a drink. As soon as they're acknowledged, the ghostly visitors will disappear. Poof. Gone.

The spirit allegedly haunting Sleepy Hollow's popular Irish pub, J.P. Doyle's, wears a uniform and a distinguishable hat.

According to one account from September 2015, a bartender named "Stacy" announced last call only to see what appeared to be a Confederate soldier emerge from the empty backyard beer garden. "The figure opened the door from the garden into the restaurant itself," reported the website *Sleepy Hollow Country*. "Exhausted from a long shift, she exclaimed, 'Oh no I'm not in the mood tonight, you've gotta go.' The figure spun around and vanished."

J.P. Doyle's "Horseman" burger was featured on the Travel Channel's *Man v. Food*. *Photo by Sam Baltrusis.*

Joni Mayhan, author of *Ghost Magnet*, told me there's a number of possible reasons why a soldier is sticking around in the afterlife. "The first thing that comes to my mind is that his haunting has more to do with the land than the actual bar," she said. "Perhaps he lived in or visited another structure that once sat on the property."

Based on the bartender's story, Mayhan believes that the soldier haunting J.P. Doyle's appears to be more residual in nature. "Perhaps this building was a tavern in his day, and he walked in every evening for a beer," she said. "The pattern was embedded into the energy of the building and continued to play out over and over again."

The author and seasoned paranormal investigator said the haunting at J.P. Doyle's reminded her of a wounded soldier spirit she encountered in room 24 at Concord's Colonial Inn in Massachusetts. "Every time we tried to engage him, he disappeared. If he had responded to us, we would have classified him as an intelligent haunting, but he didn't," Mayhan said. "His presence was recorded into the energy of the building and it preserved his memory."

Mayhan pointed out that the bartender swore she had a face-to-face encounter with a Civil War–era man in uniform. But why would a Confederate soldier be in Tarrytown?

In the early 1800s, there were a small number of farms in the area that grew mostly wheat coupled with taverns and shops that catered to the workers at Frederick Philipse's two gristmills. The economy in Tarrytown was primarily agrarian, and during the Civil War the leaders of Westchester County surprisingly had a firm stance against Abraham Lincoln.

"Westchester more than any other county in the state was divided in sentiments to South and North," said Vernon Benjamin, author of *The History of the Hudson River Valley from Wilderness to the Civil War*. "The county was a sort of Mason-Dixon line for the state, running roughly through Tarrytown."

As the Civil War erupted, plenty of men enlisted even though they were not fond of Lincoln and his politics. "They didn't feel that they were fighting for abolition," said historian Patrick Raftery in the September 30, 2015 edition of *Westchester* magazine. "They were more likely to describe themselves as fighting to preserve the Union."

For those looking for more "boos" with their brews, the bartender who spotted the Confederate soldier spirit also worked at Tarrytown's other haunted tavern, the Set Back Inn.

According to Jim Logan's article in *Sleepy Hollow Country*, the employee known as "Stacy" had an encounter with "a black-haired man wearing dark blue jeans and a black shirt leaning against the end of the bar watching as she batched out at the end of her shift," he reported. "Two patrons at the bar saw nothing, but one confirmed that odd things happen in the place. Stacy received the impression from the figure that he may have been a former Set Back bartender in the 1980s who was rumored to be a murder victim."

Set Back Inn has been a neighborhood watering hole on Main Street in Tarrytown since 1959. However, the space reportedly dates to the mid-1800s and was a popular hangout when North Tarrytown was home to a massive General Motors assembly plant.

"Like many of Main Street's buildings, this one dates to the late 1800s and is built of locally fired Hudson River red brick," Logan continued. "Saturated as it is with local history, could this unassuming local dive be home to a spirit?"

Yes, Mayhan is convinced the Set Back Inn is haunted. In fact, the author insisted that many spirits are attracted to bars and taverns because they don't want the party to ever end.

"When people die, they sometimes choose their own afterlife instead of crossing over into the white light and leaving it up to fate to decide what happens to them," she said. "As a paranormal investigator and medium, I've actually investigated quite a few bars and social clubs."

If the Set Back Inn's resident spirit was murdered, she said, there are a variety of reasons why he would remain earthbound instead of moving on.

"I believe the majority of souls cross directly over, but some balk at the time of their death and refuse to move into the light," she said. "Perhaps they have a family they want to watch over or property that they loved. Sometimes, they even stick around to guard their former business, believing that nobody else could manage it like they did. In this case, his traumatic death probably also played a role."

The allegedly haunted Set Back Inn is located at 33 Main Street in Tarrytown. *Photo courtesy of Andy Kazie from iStock.*

If the "black-haired man" haunting the Set Back Inn died suddenly in the general vicinity of the tavern, it's possible he's trapped in what is known as a ghost loop.

"In some instances, they don't even know they're dead," she explained. "They're stuck in their death state for all of eternity, playing out the murder over and over again."

Another possibility, Mayhan said, is that he's seeking postmortem justice or he simply enjoyed the vibe at the Set Back Inn during his lifetime. "Could he be trying to inform others about who killed him? Or maybe he's simply chosen this location because it was a place where he was the happiest during his life," Mayhan said. "There are too many possible scenarios to nail one down without further investigation. My hope is that someone gets to the bottom of it and helps him cross over."

TARRYTOWN MUSIC HALL

The show must go on—even in the afterlife. Talk to anyone who has worked backstage at a theatrical venue, and they'll have a ghost story or two of a close encounter with a playhouse phantom. For some reason, spirits love live theater.

Armed with dozens of refurbished historic performance structures scattered throughout the Hudson River Valley, the spellbound region is no exception to the "house ghost" rule. "The hard part isn't finding theaters that are haunted—it's finding theaters that aren't," joked Tom Ogden, author of *Haunted Theaters*.

For more than a century, the Tarrytown Music Hall on Main Street has experienced all sorts of paranormal activity since raising its curtain for the first time on December 12, 1885.

"Lights mysteriously turn back on after closing. The eerie sound of an unknown singer performing vocal scales in the wings after hours," reported the *Haunted History Trail of New York State*'s website. "High-profile artists refusing to stay in one particular dressing room because they sensed a presence."

Why haunted theaters? Author Holly Nadler believes it's the romantic aesthetic. "All old and beautiful theaters look haunted, with their shadowy corridors, flickering lanterns, vaulted ceilings, and Gothic ornaments," she wrote. "They also sound haunted, from the creaking of woodwork, the rustling of old pipes, the sighs of air currents trapped inside thick stone walls. And indeed, there are some who contend that all old and beautiful theaters really are haunted."

Angela Artuso from Gotham Paranormal investigated Tarrytown Music Hall several times in 2019. She told me that her team experienced a combination of both residual and intelligent-type hauntings.

"During our investigations there, we picked up singing, music playing, shadow figures and even a full-body apparition," she said. "I feel that the music hall has a few of its regular spirits that call it home. There are several performers who prepare and warm up for a show in the dressing room, and staff members who passed away years ago still check up on things to make sure everything is running smoothly."

In addition to the ghostly thespians, Artuso believes there are former stagehands working in the afterlife to make sure everything is set up properly. "Tarrytown Music Hall is well over one hundred years old and has been home to many performers and continues to be to this day," she said.

The backstage area seems to be the theater's most paranormally active according to Artuso. "The old production manager said it was haunted. He always heard voices and had strange experiences backstage. One night he was locking up and heard the house manager singing," she said. "The

Tarrytown Music Hall is a brick structure in the Queen Anne architectural style erected in the late 1800s. *Photo courtesy of Brian Logan Photo from Depositphotos.*

next day he told her she had a nice voice but was surprised to learn that it wasn't her. She was already gone for the day, so no one among the living was there. A piano has also been heard playing. It has been reported that unexplainable voices have been heard in response to staff making performance calls."

Artuso told me there was a feeling of uneasiness in the upper-level dressing room when her team investigated the music hall.

"Equipment has been known to go on and off as well as tip over from no known cause. After a performance, the production director was on stage putting things away along with another staff member when they heard men talking from the direction of one of the dressing rooms," she explained. "They also heard what sounded like someone singing as if they were getting warmed up before a performance. When they went to look, no one was there."

The paranormal investigator said that lights inexplicably turned on when the theater was shut down for the night. "Staff have reported seeing a light turn back on in the dressing room from the parking lot after the building had been locked for the evening and everyone had left for the day," she said.

There are also disembodied whistles heard throughout the theater. "One of the staff members who passed away used to always whistle while he worked," she said. "The whistling could also be from staff members who worked at the music hall over the years but are now long gone."

Artuso said that whistling was an invaluable tool for theater stagehands before modern communication devices such as headsets and walkie-talkies.

From the stage, there have been reports of shadow figures spotted in the projection room and the balcony when they were unoccupied. "There was also a sighting of what appeared to be a man standing on a ladder and fixing the lights on the side of the balcony," she added.

During one of their more memorable investigations, Gotham Paranormal heard the phantom chords of a piano and what sounded like a xylophone coming from the basement. Artuso also noticed the sandbags and pulley systems on the stage swing back and forth without a reasonable explanation.

The founder of Gotham Paranormal told me that one of the creepiest experiences she had at the Tarrytown Music Hall was watching a man walk

In 1980, Tarrytown Music Hall was listed on the National Register of Historic Places. *Photo courtesy of Brian Logan Photo from Depositphotos.*

into the theater and then disappear. "When everyone quickly glanced and asked each other who that was, we turned and the man was completely gone," she said. "We felt that the apparition could have been one of the older staff members who was well-loved and passed away several years ago."

Or it could have been Henry Dodge Estabrook, a Republican presidential candidate, who unexpectedly died in the theater on December 22, 1917, while watching a black-and-white motion picture. According to the *New York Sun*, he died of "heart disease super induced by acute indigestion." Estabrook was sixty-three years old.

Artuso said it's difficult to pinpoint the names responsible for the ghostly activity because of the number of people who come through the doors each year. However, she's optimistic that more information about the theater's resident spirits will emerge because they are now offering ghost tours in October.

"Its haunted reputation isn't a recent development, but the staff's willingness to embrace the theater's paranormal activity is," she told me. "Whether you're a skeptic or a believer, the Tarrytown Music Hall promises an unforgettable experience filled with history, culture and perhaps some unexplainable happenings during your visit."

CHAPTER 6

THE WATERFRONT

I f one takes a hard look at the Hudson River's legends and lore using a modern lens, there's an underlying attempt to dehumanize those who were deemed as "others" by the status quo.

Leanna Renee Hieber, coauthor of *A Haunted History of Invisible Women*, said there was a fundamental distrust of outsiders, as illustrated with the fictional Ichabod Crane and, of course, the headless Hessian in "The Legend of Sleepy Hollow."

"Throughout the American Revolution, whether patriot or loyalist, there was still a shared language," she said. "The Hessians were well-trained German-speaking mercenaries, hired guns often made out to be grim and bloodthirsty. Anxieties and traumas about the Revolution could be more easily placed onto the shoulders of a barbaric mercenary as an invading, vengeful foreigner."

Hieber told me that Hessian forces made up nearly one-quarter of the British troop placement throughout most of the American Revolution. "They were responsible for decisive victories, especially in the northern New York fronts, so their shadow looming large over areas like Tarrytown does have a fearsome historical precedent," she said.

In addition to the demonization of the Hessians, Hieber pointed out the stereotypical representation of women like the "Bronze Lady" or the "Lady in White" in local lore. The colorful ladies lacked any identifiable personality traits because their stories were often created by men in power who then controlled their narrative.

The scenic view facing Sleepy Hollow, New York, from the Hudson River. *Photo courtesy of Andy Kazie from Depositphotos.*

"Women were subsumed by their husbands, existing as second-class citizens until the 1900s," Hieber explained. "Records of women's lives are often harder to find and trace than historical accounts of men."

Hieber said Sleepy Hollow's invisible women were presented as one-dimensional amalgams rather than multifaceted people. "It's an acknowledgement of women as part of the spirit-world fabric but they tend to remain firmly in the realm of vaporous metaphor," she said. "These women of other hues may differentiate themselves by a certain context of their environment or surroundings, each hue evoking a different emotional resonance, but they're still not given names."

Alex Matsuo, author of *Women of the Paranormal*, agreed on many levels with Hieber's assessment. She believes, however, there's something a bit off-kilter with what appears to be an over-the-top fascination with women in folklore.

"Perhaps it's because they lived in a society that went above and beyond to repress them, and giving them some sort of identification or story in life is society's way to apologize," she said. "Depending on the story though, it's usually a continuation of that repression from the patriarchy."

In addition to the representation of women in local legends, Matsuo expressed concern with the portrayal of Native Americans and how they supposedly cursed the entire Hudson River Valley.

"Given how Indigenous people had their land pretty much stolen from them, this is a way to dehumanize and 'other' them in a way to justify and validate how they were treated," Matsuo told me.

Washington Irving notoriously wrote about the alleged Native American witchery in "The Legend of Sleepy Hollow."

"An old Indian chief, the prophet or wizard of his tribe, held his powwows there before the country was discovered by Master Hendrick Hudson," Irving wrote. "Certain it is, the place still continues under the sway of some witching power, that holds a spell over the minds of the good people, causing them to walk in a continual sense of reverie."

According to the October 4, 2014 edition of the *New York Post*, there was a full-blown curse on the land when colonists leveled a sacred mound. "Dutch settlers in Sleepy Hollow were eager to plant their wheat in an open field—which happened to be a Native American burial ground," wrote Mackenzie Dawson in the *Post*. "A local Weckquaesgeek chief tried to warn them away from it."

Of course, the Dutch didn't listen to the heads-up and ended up plowing the field anyway.

While there's no word if the supposed curse worked, the actual location of the burial ground is up for debate. "Some believe it was located in what is now the abandoned GM plant in Sleepy Hollow, while others say it's where Philipse Manor Metro-North station stands," the *Post* reported.

Matsuo said the Native American burial ground trope is the oldest trick in the book when it comes to "othering" the land's original inhabitants.

"Instead of perceiving these people as actual people with agency and autonomy over their land, this trope reduces them to angry people wanting to unleash magical vengeance on innocent people who did something as simple as live on their land," she said. "But it's much more complicated than that."

With that being said, there is evidence that the Hudson Valley's Indigenous people did perform protection rituals to ward off attacks from the Mohawks. In fact, famed English occultist Aleister Crowley tapped into the energy when he camped out on the nearby Esopus Island for more than a month in 1918.

But did he pick up on a lingering hex?

"Some of the early stories of the Native Americans show that those who lived along the Hudson used various conjuring tricks, warning off the Mohawks by casting spells on them," reported Jonathan Kruk in his book *Legends and Lore of Sleepy Hollow and the Hudson Valley*. "I think Crowley sensed

The Sleepy Hollow Lighthouse is a sparkplug design located on the east side of the Hudson River. *Photo courtesy of appalachianview from Depositphotos.*

there was more than just the landscape contributing to the atmosphere you feel in certain pockets around here."

Rituals were performed, but it was more of a defensive measure. No curse.

Matsuo told me there's a reason why the intentions of marginalized people have often been twisted throughout history. "Scapegoating makes it easier for us to handle horrific events," she said. "Ghost stories give us a safety filter to process the traumatic events of our nation without necessarily having to face it head on."

ARMOUR-STINER OCTAGON HOUSE

Based purely on its eerie design, the Armour-Stiner Octagon House—situated on a bluff above the Hudson River in Irvington, New York—looks haunted. According to both the current and past owners of the property, it's teeming with ghostly activity.

They swear that at least one of the lovelorn spirits from its tragic past still lingers around the structure built by Paul J. Armour in 1860 and remodeled in 1872 by a wealthy tea merchant, Joseph Stiner.

"For some odd reason, even-sided octagon shaped houses are prone to hauntings," wrote Lynda Lee Macken in *Haunted Houses of the Hudson Valley*. "Irvington's is no exception."

The ghost lore began with tenants after Stiner's renovation when a woman from France and her daughter moved in. "The beautiful girl immediately fell head over heels in love with a neighbor boy," Macken wrote. "The pair became inseparable, but their love was ill fated."

In a *Romeo and Juliet*–style twist, the parents of the boy wanted to keep the young couple apart, but the two were determined to be together and escaped from their homes with plans to take a steamship in an attempt to elope. "Under her cloak, the girl wore the wedding gown she fervently worked on each night anticipating the special day," the author continued. "The handsome sweetheart awaited her at the river's edge. Together they hurried to the dock and boarded the steamer."

The vessel ended up exploding and ultimately sinking in the Hudson River, according to the legend, and many died instantly, including the young man, while the lady in her white wedding gown tragically drowned. "The girl's mother refused the body and without delay moved back to France," Macken explained, adding that passersby often said they saw a light in the attic window, much like the candle the young woman used to communicate with her beloved before her untimely death.

Carl Carmer purchased the Armour-Stiner Octagon House in 1946 and swore by the validity of the star-crossed lovers' story until his death in 1976. "He and his wife believed they lived with spirits who often announced their

The Armour-Stiner Octagon House is a domed Victorian-style house located at 45 West Clinton Avenue in Irvington, New York. *Photo by Sam Baltrusis.*

presence with discernable scents," Macken wrote. "On some evenings, the aroma of sweet tobacco wafted down the staircase and into the parlor, its origins unknown."

According to Emily Faber's article published by the Sinclair Broadcast Group on October 20, 2021, the Lady in White made her first ghostly appearance to her mother "who was waiting angrily in the driveway for her daughter's tardy return." It could explain why she quickly packed her bags and fled back to France.

Carmer also encountered a full-bodied apparition of the Lady in White and "described seeing the woman floating down the driveway late at night," Faber wrote.

Joseph Pell Lombardi, the renowned preservation architect who took on the daunting challenge of restoring the Armour-Stiner Octagon House in 1978, and his son, Michael, didn't believe in ghosts until they both experienced several strange incidents that they couldn't explain.

"The ghost has also been credited with saving the life of a carpenter who forgot to clip in his rope while replacing the dome's slate," Faber wrote. "And my tour guides described a much more recent incident of candlesticks being knocked to the ground in what is said to be the ghost's favorite room on the building's third floor."

Both Lombardi and his son have experienced some resistance from the Armour-Stiner Octagon House's ghosts during renovations.

"While working in one of the bedrooms, Joseph stepped away from a painted-shut window to grab his toolbox and returned to find it wide open," Faber explained. "Michael, too, had a story involving tools, in which a tape measure inexplicably flew out of his bag and landed at the top of the staircase on the third floor. He also still ruminates on the footsteps that he heard while biking around the house's wrap-around veranda as a child, the source of which remains a mystery to this day."

Michael, who currently lives in the property's carriage house with his family, told Faber he's seen what he believed was the Lady in White. "Out of the corner of my eye, I will see a glimpse in another room or something passing," he said. "I'll be doing something, and I'll take pause."

After a recent "Myths & Mysteries" tour, I spoke with Michael about his experiences growing up at the Armour-Stiner Octagon House over almost five decades. He confirmed a lot of the details about the property mentioned in Faber's article, including his personal experiences with its resident spirit.

"I'm not a big believer in ghosts; however, I've had numerous unexplainable experiences here at the house," Lombardi told me. "Many visitors and workers have had experiences as well. She usually comes in the form of a fragrance of lilac or as an apparition that I have seen out of the corner of my eye."

Joni Mayhan, author of *Signs of Spirits*, told me that there are a variety of ways ghosts show their presence, including a recognizable scent. "Some of them will talk to us across our equipment; others show themselves to unsuspecting visitors," Mayhan said. "Still others will utilize a specific aroma to provide a hint of their existence. This resonates with me because the sense of smell is the sense that is the most strongly connected to memory."

Mayhan said that "perfume is especially alluring because many people like having their own signature scent."

During the "Myths & Mysteries" tour on Halloween day, Lombardi's staff had scare props set up throughout the house, including a gas-powered rocking chair in the solarium, a door that opened and closed on its own on the second floor and a spooky sheet ghost on a pulley in the attic when guests climbed up the creaky wooden stairs to the third floor.

Kathy, our tour guide at the Armour-Stiner Octagon House, talked about her personal experiences with the Lady in White, including lights that mysteriously turned on and off by themselves and objects moving on their own. In fact, she recently had a coffee mug that mysteriously moved from the gift shop on the ground floor to a second-floor bedroom. She felt like the resident ghost was being playful with her and the staff.

In Faber's article, Michael talked about one of his tours that had to be cut short after he told the group that the Lady in White often entered the room with a lilac scent. As soon as she was mentioned, they noticed a floral smell.

"It was kind of a boisterous group, and everybody got quiet," Lombardi told Faber. "It was very awkward. The tour was over, and they all left."

BANNERMAN CASTLE

When taking the train from Tarrytown to Poughkeepsie, it's hard to miss the imposing structure in ruins lurking off the shoreline of Beacon, New York.

Bannerman Castle on Pollepel Island in the Hudson River has a storied history of ghosts, goblins and curses.

"Native Americans believed the tiny island was swarming with ghosts," wrote Lynda Lee Macken in *Haunted Houses of the Hudson Valley*. "Early Europeans thought goblins possessed the land and controlled the difficult river passage where fierce currents and unpredictable storms and winds could capsize their boats. To evaluate their mettle, sailors making their first journey up river were left at the island until the ship returned for them."

The island's problematic past didn't stop Francis Bannerman—a native of Scotland who inherited his father's military surplus business in New York City—from purchasing the Hudson River property to be used as a storage facility. Bannerman's wife, Helen, who longed to live like royalty and even fancied the idea that she once was a queen in a past life, persuaded her husband to build a castle on the island replete with a moat, drawbridge, hidden tunnels and even a dungeon. The munitions dealer began construction on a Scottish-style castle that became their summer residence in 1901.

"To build docks, Bannerman bought old ships, sunk them, and covered them with concrete," wrote Macken. One tugboat captain who was in his twilight years requested to be upriver before workers sunk his beloved vessel. They didn't wait.

"Tactlessly, the ship went down before he could even turn away," Macken wrote. "Furious with their lack of consideration, the hapless captain cursed the crew and Bannerman too."

After the upset captain's passing, workers heard what sounded like a double clang of the ship's bell, which indicated that the tugboat was in reverse. "All

Bannerman Castle, an abandoned military surplus warehouse, is located on Pollepel Island in Beacon, New York. *Photo courtesy of littleny from Depositphotos.*

attributed the ethereal ringing to the captain's angry spirit eternally backing up his boat away from the island," the author explained.

According to Macken, the island's paranormal activity seemed to increase when workers started to build the elaborate castle. "Apparitions of headless soldiers were widespread on the island in Bannerman's day."

The Manhattan-based businessman passed away in 1918, and construction of the castle was paused. However, it was just the beginning of what would become a series of odd and extremely unfortunate events.

There was also a catastrophic mishap during a routine test when ammunition accidentally fell through the roof of one of the warehouses. "An explosion ensued destroying the building as well as the unfortunate workers inside," Macken explained. "Supposedly their ghosts also haunt the island."

According to Donald Burns in his May 10, 2016 article posted on the website *Medium*, it has been rumored that the island was inhabited by Native American spirits protecting the land. Many people believed these entities were responsible for enforcing the curse.

"It is true that history could indicate that the island's situation is more than a matter of sheer bad luck, but it is inevitable to imagine that the vengeful spirits caused its decline and fall," Burns wrote. "It was thought that the explosion had been caused by lightning that struck the flagpoles. Locals must have looked at each other, thinking that the spirits were making mischief."

As Burns noted, however, the worst was yet to come. "In 1950, a cargo ship, the *Pollepel*, was in the middle of a huge storm in the Hudson River," he wrote. "It crashed on the island during the height of the storm, exploding on impact. The blast caused even more damage to the building—and the ill-fated boat gave the island its modern name, although many still call it Bannerman's Island."

Then there was a massive fire in 1969 that destroyed what remained of the elaborate structure, leaving it without ceilings and floors. The façade of the massive castle quickly fell into ruins even though it was constructed in the early 1900s. "Since then, the river has almost completely destroyed the walls of the port, leaving only the turrets and bridges surrounded by water," Burns added. "The weather has made it lose its white paint and coating and vandalism and vegetation have also contributed to gradually deteriorate the walls."

Bannerman's grandson Charles wrote about the castle's untimely demise seven years before the fire that destroyed what remained. "No one can tell what associations and incidents will involve the island in the future," he wrote. "Time, the elements, and maybe even the goblins of the island will take their toll on some of the turrets and towers, and perhaps eventually the castle itself, but the little island will always have its place in history and in legend and will forever be a jewel in its Hudson Highland setting."

While the structural integrity of Bannerman Castle quickly degraded over the years, legends associated with the property have flourished. "There are also reports that sailors believed a 'tribe of goblins' controlled the waters and wind which would cause boats sailing the Hudson River to sink," wrote Jess, an on-air radio personality at local country radio station The Wolf. "The scariest part? Some say that during big storms you can still hear the crew crying for help."

Other ghost stories include a phantom horse galloping across the once functional drawbridge and an odd whistling sound echoing throughout the property. Some visitors have heard what sounded like a nonoperational generator mysteriously turning on, and one of the superintendent's sons said his bed would levitate during overnight stays at Bannerman Castle before it became uninhabitable.

Want to experience the island's ghosts and goblins? While there currently aren't any paranormal investigations planned in the near future, there are guided walking tours available from May through October that include a boat ride from nearby Beacon, New York. Organizers even offer monthly movie nights for visitors wanting to enjoy the island's eerie aesthetic after dark, with an appropriate lineup of films including *The Ghost and Mrs. Muir*, *The Wizard of Oz* and *Hocus Pocus*.

HUDSON RIVER

Beware of the mythical creatures, spirited sailors and phantom ships lurking among the foggy mist from the Hudson River's murky waters.

According to local lore, there's an army of imps led by a goblin king on Dunderberg Mountain who "have long been suspected of whipping up sudden storms, conjuring fog in the middle of a clear day, sinking boats and swamping the canoes of those who failed to pay proper homage, either by tipping a hat or lowering a sail," reported Mackenzie Dawson in the October 4, 2014 edition of the *New York Post*.

It's tradition for sea captains traveling upriver to tip their hats to the leader of the imps—also referred to as the Heer of Dunderberg—before sailing past the deepest part of the river known as World's End.

The spellbound region stretches along the Hudson River from Westchester to Albany, New York. *Photo courtesy of deberarr from Depositphotos.*

"While the rumored river imps have been causing mischief for centuries, many New York City harbor pilots still tip their hats as they sail past the point just before the Bear Mountain Bridge—better to be safe than sorry," Dawson explained.

What did the goblin king look like? "The Dutch sailors described him as a small round imp-like creature wearing a light colored sugar-loaf hat. It is rumored that he would leave this hat on some of the ships that were under his attack. And when the ship would be in the clear, the hat would blow away," reported the *International Ghosts and Hauntings* blog.

"Sailors would tack horseshoes to the masts of their ship for good luck while sailing the Heer of Dunderberg's domain. They were truly afraid of these waters. They also had fear of seeing the ghostly 'storm ship' said to be manned by the Heer's goblin army. Once it approached, the horrific winds, thunder, lightning, and rain would bear down on a ship until it was sunk."

Andrew Warburton, author of *New England Fairies*, told me the mythology associated with the "imps of Dunderberg" was likely popularized by Washington Irving's fictional work, and in turn, the short-story writer was inspired by folklore from the Netherlands. "Irving seems to have been well-versed in Dutch fairy folklore, including tales about goblin kings who lived in mountains, like the imps of Dunderberg and other stories about goblins,"

Warburton explained. "So who knows, perhaps Irving did base his fiction on things he'd learned from the Dutch of the Hudson Valley."

Warburton said the idea that the imps can only come out after dark likely originated from the Dutch, who believed the creatures were made out of clay. "There was a saying with Bannerman Island that visitors were unlikely to encounter the river imps during the day because, apparently, they only come out at night. This is consistent with Dutch folklore in which imps and goblins cannot come out at night because the sun will turn them to stone."

In an interesting side note, one of the goblins that occupied Dunderberg Mountain reportedly followed a minister from the Old Dutch Church in Kingston as he was en route to New York City. "As the ship the minister was traveling on passed Dunderberg, sure enough, the hobgoblin sprung into action and brought on a huge storm before crawling down the mast and taking over the vessel," reported radio show host Simon from WRRV-FM in Poughkeepsie.

"The minister acted quickly and performed an exorcism to chase the hobgoblin off. But before the ghoul could be repelled, it grabbed a hat off the minister's wife's head. The hat was found the next day some 60 miles away at the minister's church in Kingston," Simon wrote.

Somehow the goblin became entrapped in the steeple at Kingston's historic Dutch Reformed Church and remains there to this day.

According to the *New York Post* article, imps and goblins aren't the only troublemakers causing havoc up and down the Hudson River.

"Some think they're seeing the *Flying Dutchman*, the ship that paid a terrible price after its captain cursed both God and the devil in order to round Cape Horn safely," reported Dawson. "They made the difficult passage, but were doomed to sail on for eternity, docking in a port just one night every seven years—unless one of the crew members could find a woman to fall in love with."

Jonathan Kruk, author of *Legends and Lore of Sleepy Hollow and Tarrytown*, told the *New York Post* that "the mists on the Hudson River have caused people to believe they're seeing a ship."

He also joked that it's possible that the ghosts of the cursed men from the *Flying Dutchman* were spotted frequenting local watering holes. "People have met odd strangers in Tarrytown bars and thought, 'Maybe these are members of the crew, trying to get someone to break the spell,'" Kruk added.

And then there are ghostly stories associated with a certain English navigator said to haunt the New York river that later bore his name.

"Legend has it that every twenty years, since 1609, Henry Hudson and his crew return to bowl ninepins with the gnomes of the Catskills Mountains," reported the *Wall Street Walks* blog. "The crash of the pins is heard in the form of thunder. Sometimes this thunder is so loud that it can be heard all the way down the Hudson River Valley in New York City."

Trapped in the ice through a long winter in the early 1600s, Hudson's crew eventually mutinied and set their captain and eight of his crewmen adrift on a makeshift vessel. The captain and his mates were never seen again.

It's said that Hudson's ghost often appears on his ship, the *Half Moon*, riding out a storm in New York Harbor.

In addition to the *Flying Dutchman* and the English explorer's ghost ship, there's a Revolutionary War–era soldier haunting the Hudson River's coastline.

Brigadier General Anthony Wayne, who carried out the order to hang British spy John André in 1780, was the commander of the Continental army forces assigned to patrol the Hudson River. "His ghost is said to haunt the riverfront but out of respect for André's ghost, it carefully avoids Patriot's Park," reported Jerry Eimbinder in the September 30, 2011 edition of *Tarrytown–Sleepy Hollow Patch*.

What does this all mean?

Warburton believes most of the over-the-top legend and lore associated with the Hudson River stems from Irving's attempt to romanticize the spellbound region.

"He clearly tapped into the dark folklore of the Hudson Valley's Dutch community, especially with stories about goblin kings residing in mountains, bands of imps terrorizing local settlements and even ghost ships like the *Flying Dutchman*," Warburton concluded.

In other words, blame it on Irving.

CONCLUSION

I f a ghost is history demanding to be remembered, then what the heck is going on in Sleepy Hollow? It appears that a lot of the reported paranormal activity from Washington Irving's stories has somehow galloped off of the page and taken on a life of its own.

The literature-inspired legend and lore includes a rogues' gallery of characters led by the ultimate villain, the Headless Horseman.

But is art imitating the spirits—or is it the other way around?

My friend and fellow author Richard Estep is the go-to guy when I need a grounded perspective in the field. When I mentioned the possibility of an egregore manifestation, he weighed in with his thoughts on the spellbound region's alleged hauntings.

"We've talked at length about thought-forms in the past," Estep said. "The key question is, how many of the sightings and encounters are the product of preexisting bias, expectation, imagination and wishful thinking—versus being objectively real?"

Estep said it's important to carefully evaluate the evidence before making the claim that it's actually paranormal. "For example, knowing the notoriously boggy, waterlogged ground in that part of the country, are hoofprints ever found or has physical contact been reported? I'm interested in whether there are any physical aspects on record," Estep said.

While there's at least one encounter involving an unseen force throwing a man over the Headless Horseman Bridge in the 1800s, the reports of the phantom rider have definitely diminished in recent years. "It sounds like a case of the battery draining over a long period of time," he said, adding that he's currently working on a book project about the Mothman sightings from the 1960s in Point Pleasant, West Virginia.

Estep pointed out the similarities between the headless Hessian and the man-sized bird.

"There are definitely a sufficient number of parallels between the two cases to make for a good comparison," he said. "If I recall correctly, sightings of the Horseman ramped up after the publication of Irving's short story."

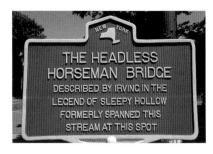

Plaque near the Old Dutch Church and Sleepy Hollow Cemetery marking the spot of the original Headless Horseman Bridge in "The Legend of Sleepy Hollow." *Photo courtesy of deberarr from Depositphotos.*

Based on the firsthand accounts in Edward Mayhew Bacon's book *Chronicles of Tarrytown and Sleepy Hollow*, there were several reports of Irving's monster soon after the story's release in 1820.

As far as contemporary encounters, not so much.

"Following the initial media flap of Mothman stories, the same happened in the wake of John Keel's book and continues to this day," he explained. "There are big-screen adaptations of each story. The Headless Horseman, however, had close to a 150-year head start over the Mothman, so it's interesting to note that he is encountered less frequently these days compared to the sightings in West Virginia."

The discussion about the alleged reports of a Horseman-inspired entity forced me to reevaluate the man behind the legend. Did Irving conjure up the lore to make the Hudson River Valley more interesting?

While he did fancy himself a historian and even penned a five-volume series on George Washington, it's hard to deny that he was somewhat of an unreliable narrator.

In fact, my opinion of Irving changed while writing *Ghosts of Sleepy Hollow*. I came into the project with "woes-colored glasses," expecting to cement my love for the trailblazing writer who inspired my idols like Nathaniel Hawthorne, Charles Dickens and even Edgar Allan Poe.

After taking a deep dive into the man's mythical backstory, I couldn't help but think that there was something inauthentic about the celebrated author. Some of his story seemed contrived, as if it was crafted in the spirit of his greatest tales.

His relationship with Matilda Hoffman? It felt almost like a façade, fabricated a bit by biographers wanting to find a heart string to the afterlife that may or may not have existed.

Morning fog sets the scene for the Headless Horseman in the spellbound region's Sleepy Hollow. *Photo courtesy of xbrchx from Depositphotos.*

Don't get me wrong, I'm still smitten with "The Legend of Sleepy Hollow," and I was able to tap into the excitement I had as a young boy thinking about the Headless Horseman roaming the wooded landscape of the Hudson Valley while writing this book.

But I wanted to idolize the man who created my all-time favorite monster. What I uncovered was someone who deeply loved his family, almost to a fault. He was needy at times and an unlikely writer who hid behind a nom de plume in order to make snarky observations about the city that never sleeps. Even though Irving was prolific, he didn't actually enjoy the writing process.

Irving was born and raised in Manhattan but traveled overseas and ultimately found his place a few miles outside of New York City in the Hudson Valley. He was always on the move, but his personal baggage always seemed to follow him.

In hindsight, I had this romantic ideal of a man I viewed as the 1800s equivalent of Stephen King. Truthfully, his backstory was much more layered and complicated than I expected.

He was a marketing genius who came up with words like *Gotham* and *Knickerbocker* that cleverly labeled his hometown and its Dutch denizens,

Doppelgänger? Author Sam Baltrusis specializes in historical haunts and has been featured on several national television shows sharing his experiences with the paranormal. *Photo by Frank C. Grace.*

respectively. Santa Claus? That was Irving's idea, years before Old Saint Nick invaded department stores and malls across the country. He was, in essence, a brand manager before the concept even existed.

Even though he inspired the generation of Gothic writers that came after him, he was never as tortured as Poe or rebellious as Hawthorne. He chose the middle road, not to veer too far off the beaten path.

After careful introspection and dissecting why my opinion changed about a writer whom I adored as a young man, many of the issues I had with Irving reflected some of the inner demons I've grappled with most of my adult life.

The Headless Horseman is merely an outward manifestation of the fears we all have: death, dying and being alone.

I identified with Irving's issues with control and feeling more like a demasculinized Ichabod Crane who was bullied by the alpha male antagonist. I wanted to be Brom Bones, but truthfully, I was more like Crane. I was always the nerdy outsider who never quite fit in.

I feel the pain in Irving's writing. I identify with his penchant for escapism and obsession with gloom and doom. Lifelong bachelorhood? Yes, that's me. Irving's story is very much my own.

My struggle to accept the truths about the famed short story writer mirrors my lifelong inability to embrace the darkness within myself. *Ghosts of Sleepy Hollow* is not only my attempt to revisit the monsters lurking in the shadows of Irving's home and local haunts in a mythical area he labeled as the spellbound region but also about accepting my authentic self.

Once I made this realization, I shivered in the beauty and the madness of the moment. While Irving wrote the story that haunted my childhood more than two hundred years ago, there's something about the man's mythical journey as a writer that hits close to home.

My true self is an amalgam of all three men in "The Legend of Sleepy Hollow": the fearful Crane, the hypermasculinized Brom Bones and even the tortured Headless Horseman destined to roam in the darkness of the collective unconscious. I am Irving.

SOURCES

T he material in this book is drawn from published sources, including my articles in *Haunted Magazine* and issues of *New York Post*, the *New York Times*, *Daily Voice*, the *Journal News*, *Sinclair Broadcast Group*, *Hudson Valley* and *Westchester* magazines, and television programs like *Scariest Places in America* on Tubi and the *Dark Shadows* series, which inspired the movies *House of Dark Shadows* and *Night of Dark Shadows*. Disney's animated classic *The Adventures of Ichabod and Mr. Toad* was also noted.

Several books on New York's paranormal history were used and cited throughout the text. Radio stations including WNYC News, The Wolf, WRRV-FM and the websites for *Haunted History Trail of New York*, *OTIS: Odd Things I've Seen*, *Sleepy Hollow Country*, *Spooky Stuff with Alex Matsuo*, *Tarrytown–Sleepy Hollow Patch*, *Week In Weird*, *Medium*, *Haunting Around America*, *Wall Street Walks*, *Haunted Places*, *International Ghosts and Hauntings*, *NYC Ghosts* and *Visit Sleepy Hollow* also served as sources.

Most of the experts featured in this book—Jonathan Kruk, J.W. Ocker, Alex Matsuo, Leanna Renee Hieber, Joni Mayhan, Richard Estep, Brian J. Cano, Christopher Rondina, Andrew Warburton, Ken Summers and Angela Artuso—are also authors, and I highly recommend their works as supplemental reading.

For the majority of *Ghosts of Sleepy Hollow*, I conducted firsthand interviews, and some of the material is drawn from my own research. Discussions with many of the guides at the various historic haunts served as major sources and generated original content. It should be noted that ghost stories are subjective, and I have made a concerted effort to stick to the historical facts, even if it resulted in debunking a legend that has been presented as fact over time.

Atteberry, Todd. *Haunted Travels in the Hudson River Valley of Washington Irving*. New York: Todd Atteberry, 2019.

Bacon, Edward Mayhew. *Chronicles of Tarrytown and Sleepy Hollow*. New York: Knickerbocker Press, 1897.

Baltrusis, Sam. *Ghosts of Boston: Haunts of the Hub*. Charleston, SC: The History Press, 2012.

———. *Ghosts of Salem: Haunts of the Witch City*. Charleston, SC: The History Press, 2014.

———. *Ghosts of the American Revolution*. Guilford, CT: Globe Pequot Press, 2021.

———. *Ghost Writers: The Hallowed Haunts of Unforgettable Literary Icons*. Guilford, CT: Globe Pequot Press, 2019.

———. *Haunted Boston Harbor*. Charleston, SC: The History Press, 2016.

Benjamin, Vernon. *The History of the Hudson River Valley from Wilderness to the Civil War*. New York: Harry N. Abrams, 2014.

Bradley, Elizabeth L. *Knickerbocker: The Myth Behind New York*. New Brunswick, NJ: Rivergate Books, 2009.

Haughton, Brian. *Lore of the Ghost*. Franklin Lakes, NJ: Career Press, 2008.

Hauk, Dennis William. *Haunted Places: The National Directory*. New York: Penguin Group, 1996.

Hieber, Leanna Renee, and Andrea Janes. *A Haunted History of Invisible Women*. New York: Kensington Publishing, 2022.

Holzer, Hans. *This House Is Haunted*. New York: Black Dog & Leventhal Publishers, 1997.

Irving, Washington. *The Sketch Book of Geoffrey Crayon, Gent.* Oxford, UK: Oxford University Press, 2009.

Kruk, Jonathan. *Legends and Lore of Sleepy Hollow and the Hudson Valley*. Charleston, SC: The History Press, 2011.

Macken, Lynda Lee. *Haunted Houses of the Hudson Valley*. Forked River, NJ: Black Cat Press, 2022.

Mayhan, Joni. *Dark and Scary Things*. Gardner, MA: Joni Mayhan, 2015.

Nadler, Holly Mascott. *Ghosts of Boston Town: Three Centuries of True Hauntings*. Camden, ME: Down East Books, 2002.

Ocker, J.W. *The New York Grimpendium. A Guide to Macabre and Ghastly Sites*. Taftsville, VT: Countryman Press, 2012.

Owens, William A. *Pocantico Hills, 1609–1959.* Tarrytown, NY: Sleepy Hollow Restorations, 1960.

Rondina, Christopher. *Legends of Sleepy Hollow.* Newport, RI: Ghost Boy Press, 2019.

Tucker, Elizabeth. *Haunted Halls: Ghostlore of American College Campuses.* Jackson: University Press of Mississippi, 2007.

Zwicker, Roxie J. *Haunted Pubs of New England: Raising Spirits of the Past.* Charleston, SC: The History Press, 2007.

ABOUT THE AUTHOR

am Baltrusis, author of *Ghosts of Salem: Haunts of the Witch City* and featured in *The Curse of Lizzie Borden* shock doc, has penned eighteen paranormal-themed books, including *Haunted Boston Harbor* and *Ghosts of the American Revolution*. He has been featured on several national TV shows, including the Travel Channel's *A Haunting, Most Terrifying Places, Haunted Towns* and *Fright Club* (1 and 2). He also made a cameo in the documentary *The House in Between 2* and on several additional television programs, including *The UnBelievable with Dan Aykroyd, History's Most Haunted, Paranormal Nightshift* and *Forbidden History*. Baltrusis is a sought-after lecturer who speaks at libraries and paranormal-related events across the country.

Visit SamBaltrusis.com for more information.

Above: Sam Baltrusis, author of *Ghosts of Sleepy Hollow*, visits the Headless Horseman statue located between Philipsburg Manor and the Old Dutch Church. *Photo courtesy of Sam Baltrusis.*

FREE eBOOK OFFER

Scan the QR code below, enter your e-mail address and get our original Haunted America compilation eBook delivered straight to your inbox for free.

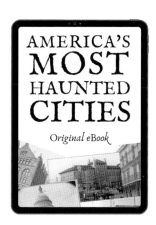

ABOUT THE BOOK

Every city, town, parish, community and school has their own paranormal history. Whether they are spirits caught in the Bardo, ancestors checking on their descendants, restless souls sending a message or simply spectral troublemakers, ghosts have been part of the human tradition from the beginning of time.

In this book, we feature a collection of stories from five of America's most haunted cities: Baltimore, Chicago, Galveston, New Orleans and Washington, D.C.

SCAN TO GET
AMERICA'S MOST HAUNTED CITIES

Having trouble scanning? Go to:
biz.arcadiapublishing.com/americas-most-haunted-cities

Visit us at
www.historypress.com